THE THEORY OF INDIAN CLASSICAL DANCE

(JUNIOR AND SENIOR EXAM)

DR. MEGHNA VENKAT

ISBN 979-8-89322-721-5

Hari Om

TABLE OF CONTENTS

PREFACE

I originally wrote this book with my students in mind, for whom I used to administer yearly examinations at my institute. I discovered later, when they were taking the Junior Senior examinations, that there weren't many books on this subject accessible in the market. Hence, I complied according to the syllabus so they could study for the exams. I then made the decision to release the book. It took some time, but eventually the book made its way out. I am appreciative of my students at Nritya Nadam Vidhyalaya since they never cease to motivate me.

Nothing in work comes together effortlessly. Completing a project is usually an enormous undertaking, and this book is no exception. Several people contribute along the road for its implementation.

I am indebted to my Guru, Sri Adyar K Lakshman sir, for his wisdom and direction. I am grateful to all of my mentors and Acharyas, whose guidance helped me develop an ideal way of understanding.

I am truly grateful to my parents for shaping who I am today. My love to my husband and our son Rishikesh, who trusted my efforts. I also want to thank my entire family for their inspiration and support.

This book is for all of you, who want to delve into the poetry of classical dance and explore its fascinating insights.

JUNIOR EXAM SYLLABUS

<u>Theory</u>

Various classical dances of India

Lakshanas or definitions of Sabha, patra apaatra, kinkini, natyakrama.

Legends of Bharatanatyam

Architecture in dance

Music in dance

Literary works on dance

Origin of dance

<u>Oral</u>

Dasavidha adavus

Chaturvidha abhinaya

Navarasa

Sapta thala

Hasta mudra

Shiro bheda, dhristi bheda, greeva bheda and bhru bheda

Five jaathis of thala

Practical

Paper 1

Identification of hasta mudra and telling usage (without sloka)

Description of allarippu, jathiswaram and devernama.

Music (singing) – sarali varise – 7, Janti varise – 5, alankara – 7, Geethe – 4

Paper 2

Exercise and Aasana

Adavu in Trikala jathi (to be recited by the student)

Bhedas

With accompaniment of teacher:-

To perform allarippu

To perform jathiswaram

To perform devernama

(Knowledge of its thala, raga, composer and its meaning)

CHAPTER 01

THE CLASSICAL DANCE FORMS OF INDIA

BHARATANATYAM:

Bharatanatyam is a dance of Tamil Nadu. This dance follows the rules of Natyasastra by Bharatamuni and it follows the book Nandikeshwara's Abhinaya Darpana. Bharatanatyam is known for its grace, purity, strength, expressions and poses. We find mention of Bharatanatyam during the sangam period in Tholkapiyam and Silapadikaram during which time dance flourished. Bharatanatyam has three distinct elements Nritta (pure dance/rhythmic steps), Natya (Dramatic expressions) and Nritya (combination of steps and expressions). There are several styles in Bharatanatyam such as Tanjavur, Pandanallur, Kalakshetra, Mysuru, Vazhuvar. The Tanjore Quartet – Chinnaiah, Ponnaiah, Shivananda and Vadivelu wrote many songs and established various centres of learning during the Maratha king, Sharobji Maharaj. This period made a rich contribution to music and dance. They also re-edited the bharatanatyam format to its present shape which is known as the margam. The margam begins with Allarippu, Jathiswaram, Shabdham, Varnam, Padam/Javali, Thillana. The jewellery used is called temple jewellery, which has red stones called kemp and green stones called paccha with gold plated on silver jewellery. Some of the jewelleries are thalai samaan (head sets), waist belt, chains, bangles etc. Dancers wear anklets tied with the help of leather or cloth belt with rows of copper bells attached to it. The costumes are heavy, pure (Kancheepuram) silk sarees. The music for Bharatanatyam is carnatic music. The instruments which are accompanied includes mridangam, flute, violin, veena, nattuvangam or cymbols. Sometimes Nagaswaram and tavil are also used. A dancer must demonstrate a number of qualities like egility, steadiness, intelligence, devotion, conversant with the sixty four types of arts and crafts and singing. The word bharatanatyam is derived from the combination of Bhavam (BHA), ragam (RA) and thalam (THA) – BhaRaTha. The original names of bharatnatyam were sadir nritya, chinna melam and dasi attam. Few exponents and Gurus of Bharatanatyam are Padma Subramanyam, C V Chandrasekhar, Adyar K Lakshman, Balasaraswathi, Saroja Vaidyanathan, U S Krishna Rao.

The Kings who patronised & promoted Bharatanatayam are Raja Raja chola, King Somadeva, Hoysala King Vishnuvardhana (wife Shanthala Devi), Krishna Deva Raya, Tulajaj, Sarabhoji, Mysore King Krishnaraja Wodeyar, Maharaja Swathi Tirunal, Mummadi Krishna Raja Wodeyar, Chamaraja Wodeyar, Jayachamaraja Wodeyar.

KUCHIPUDI:

Kuchipudi is a dance form of Andhra Pradesh. It developed from dance dramas from 15th century, for eg Bhama kalapam, prahalada charitam. It was practiced in the village 'Kuchipudi' of Krishna district. Brahmins were primarily practicing this dance form. In the olden days only men performed this style but in recent times women also perform. The performance usually begins with stage rites or purva ranga after which each character is introduced by a sutra dhara (narrator), set the mood then the dance drama begins. This dance is accompanied by carnatic music. Instruments used are mridangam, flute, violin, veena, nattuvangam or cymbols. Ornaments worn by the artists are generally made of light weight wood called 'booruju'. It originated in the 7th century but now a days temple jewellery is worn. The hairdo is very eloborate with a long plait which is worn in the front. The anklets are copper bells tied to a small rope.

In the 13th century, the importance to kuchipudi was given by Sidhendra Yogi. Siddhendra Yogi redefined the dance form. There are several items performed in Kuchipudi, both abhinaya and nritta pieces. Tarangam is a unique item performed in Kuchipudi. In this the dancer holds a plate with two diyas (small oil-burning candles) in her hands while balancing a "kindi" (small vessel) containing water. They do steps on a brass plate to the rhythmic patterns of the song. The song accompanying this number is taken from the well known Krishna Leela Tarangini, composed by Saint Narayana Theertha, a text which recounts the life and events of Lord Krishna. In expressional numbers a dancer sometimes chooses to enact the role of Satyabhama, the proud and self-assured queen of Lord Krishna, from the dance-drama Bhama Kalapam.

One more item from the Kuchipudi repertoire that deserves mention is Krishna Shabdam, in which a milkmaid invites Krishna for a rendezvous in various ways giving full scope for the dancer to display the charms of a woman.

The dance style is based on the standard treatises, Abhinaya Darpana and Bharatarnava of Nandikeshwara. (*Extra information: – The dance is sub-divided into Nattuva Mala and Natya Mala. Nattuva Mala is of two types — the Puja dance performed on the*

Balipitha in the temple and the Kalika dance performed in a Kalyana Mandapam. Natya Mala is of three kinds — ritual dance for gods, Kalika dance for intellectuals and Bhagavatam for common place. The Natya Mala is a dance-drama performed by a troupe, consisting only of men, who play feminine roles.)

The graceful, lasya oriented Kuchipudi gives importance to Vakyartha abhinaya. Bharatanatyam on the other hand is Mudra oriented and gives importance to Padartha abhinaya, each word interpreted through mudras. In Kuchipudi the dancer interprets the entire sentence into her abhinaya. Vachika abhinaya (use of words/dialogues) is a special feature of the Kuchipudi style.

From the later part of the fourth decade of this century a sequence of the presentation of the solo recital has been widely accepted. A recital of Kuchipudi begins with an invocatory number, **Ganesha Vandana**. Followed by usually *jatiswaram*. Next presented is a narrative number called **shabdam**. The *Shabdam* is followed by a **natya** number called **Kalaapam**. Many Kuchipudi dancers prefer to perform entry of Satyabhama from the traditional dance-drama Bhaamaakalaapam. *(Extra Information: – The song "bhamane, satyabhamane, the traditional **praveshadaaru** (the song that is rendered at the time of the entry of a character))*

Next in the sequence comes a pure nritya abhinaya number like **padam, jaavli, shlokam,** etc. A Kuchipudi recital is usually concluded with tarangam.

Some notable names are Lakshmi Narayana Sastry gaaru, Vempati Chinna Satyam, C.R. Acharyalu, and Dr. Nataraja Ramakrishna, Raja Radha Reddy, Vyjayanthi Kashi.

ODISSI:

Odissi, also known as **Orissi**, is one of the eight classical dance forms of India. It originates from the state of Odisha, in eastern India. It is the oldest surviving dance form of India on the basis of archaeological evidences.

It is particularly distinguished from other classical Indian dance forms by the importance it places upon the Tribhangi (literally: three parts break), the independent movement of head, chest and pelvis and upon the basic square stance known as Chauka or Chouka that symbolises Lord Jagannath. This dance is characterised by various Bhangas (Stance), The common Bhangas are Bhanga Abanga, Atibhanga and tribhanga.

Though a very old dance form, Odissi got recognition as a classical dance from the Central government after tremondous efforts taken by many scholars and performers in the 1950s, including a powerful lec-dem in April 1958 by Kavichandra Kalicharan Pattanayak, an Oriya poet, dramatist and researcher. Pattanayak is also credited with naming the dance form as "Odissi".

Odissi was initially performed in the temples as a religious offering by the Maharis who dedicated their lives in the services of God. It has the closest resemblance with sculptures of the Indian temples.

Orissa follows the Natya Sastra by Bharata Muni and Abhinaya Chandrika written by Maheshvara Mahapatra.

The Odissi tradition existed in three schools: *Mahari, Nartaki,* and *Gotipua.*

- **Maharis** were the Oriya devadasis or temple girls. They mostly perform on the lyrics of Jayadeva's Gita Govindam.

- By the 6th century, the **Gotipua** tradition was emerging. Gotipuas were boys dressed up as girls to perform.

- **Nartaki** dance took place in the royal courts, where it was much cultivated before the British period.

The traditional repertoire of Orissi is Mangalacharan, Battu Nritya, Pallavi, Abhinaya, Moksha nritta.

Odissi dance is accompanied by Odissi music, a synthesis of four classes of music i.e. Dhruvapada, Chitrapada, Chitrakala and Panchal. The instruments used are Pakhawaj, the bansuri (flute), the manjira (metal cymbals), the sitar and the tanpura.

The jewellery is made from intricate filigree silver jewellery. They wear eloborate waist band, long and short chains, bangles, ear rings and white jasmine flowers on the hair which is shaped in a half moon shape. The anklets are tied in a small rope. Sambalpuri Saree and Bomkai Saree is used for performance with Odisha prints on it.

Kelucharan Mohapatra, Pankaj Charan Das, Deba Prasad Das and Raghunath Dutta were the four major gurus who revived Odissi in the late forties and early fifties. Few other dancers are Shoren Lowen, Mayadhar Raut, Ranjana Gauhar.

KATHAKALI:

Kathakali is a classical Indian dance-drama of Kerala noted for the attractive make-up of characters, elaborate costumes, detailed gestures and well-defined body movements presented in tune with the music and complementary percussion. This dance originated in 17th century.

Vallathol Narayana Menon is credited with revitalising Kathakali. The revival of the art of Kathakali in modern Kerala was mainly due to the efforts of Vallathol and the Kerala Kalamandalam.

According to tradition, there are 101 classical Kathakali stories, though less than a third of these are commonly staged at present. Almost all of them were initially composed to last a whole night. Now a days it is performed for shorter duration. Kathakali is usually performed in front of the huge Kalivilakku (kali meaning dance; vilakku meaning lamp).

(Extra Information: – Some of the popular stories enacted are Nalacharitham (a story from the Mahabharata), Duryodhana Vadham (focusing on the Mahabharata war after profiling the build-up to it), Kalyanasougandhikam (the story of Bhima going to get flowers for his wife Panchali), Keechakavadham (another story of Bhima and Panchali, but this time during their stint in disguise), kuchelavrittam, Dakshayagam, Poothana moksham.)

The language of the songs used for Kathakali is **Manipravalam**. Though most of the songs are set in ragas based on the Carnatic music, there is a distinct style of plain-note rendition, which is known as the Sopanam style.

The percussion instruments used are chenda, maddalam and at times edakka.

*(**Extra Information:** – A Kathakali actor uses immense concentration, skill and physical stamina, gained from regimented training based on Kalaripayattu, the ancient martial art of Kerala, to prepare for his demanding role. The story is enacted purely by the movements of the hands or mudras and by facial expressions (rasas) and bodily movements. The expressions are derived from Natyashastra and are classified into nine as in most Indian classical art forms. Dancers also undergo special practice sessions to learn control of their eye, cheek and chin movements.)*

One of the most interesting aspects of Kathakali is its elaborate make-up code. Most often, the make-up can be classified into five basic sets namely Pachcha, Kathi, Kari, Thaadi, and Minukku. The differences between these sets lie in the predominant colours that are applied on the face. Pachcha (meaning green) has green as the dominant colour and is used to portray noble male characters who are said to have "Satvik" (pious) nature. Minukku is generally for women and is painted in red and yellow. Kathi is for Rajasik roles and is painted with red and green. Thadi is divided into three categories – veluppu portrays Hanuman, Chokkana portraying Aggressive roles, Karupu portrays devil roles like Kiratha. Kari is used for Women demons like Puthana.

Senior Kathakali exponents of today include Padma Bhushan Kalamandalam Ramankutty Nair, Padma Shri Kalamandalam Gopi, Madavoor Vasudevan Nair, Chemancheri Kunhiraman Nair, Kottakkal Krishnankutty Nair.

MOHINIATTAM:

Mohiniattam is a classical dance of Kerala which originated in the 16th century. It is considered a graceful form of Kerala meant to be performed as solo recitals by women.

The word "Mohiniyattam" literally means *"dance of the enchantress"*. The name Mohiniyattam may have been coined after Lord Vishnu. The main theme of the dance is love and devotion to God, with usually Vishnu or Krishna being the hero. Devadasis used to perform this in temples. It also has elements of Koothu and Kottiyattom.

Mohiniyattam was popularized as a popular dance form in the nineteenth century by Swathi Thirunal, the Maharaja of the state of Travancore (Southern Kerala), and Vadivelu, one of the Thanjavur Quartet. The noted Malayalam poet Vallathol, who established the Kerala Kalamandalam dance school in 1930, played an important role in popularizing Mohiniattam in the 20th century. Smt. Kalamandalam Kalyanikutty Amma (considered "the mother of Mohiniyattam")—contributed to the shaping out of the contemporary Mohiniyattam. *(Extra Information: – The first reference to Mohiniyattam is found in 'Vyavaharamala' composed by Mazhamangalam Narayanan Namboodiri, of 16th century AD. Major contributions to this art form were also given by Irayimman Thampi and Kuttikunju Thankachi.)*

There are approximately 40 basic movements, known as atavukal. The dance has a lot of swaying and gentle movements. The performer uses the eyes to convey all her expressions. In the main items Cholkettu, Padavarnam and Padam – Mudras and facial expressions are more important than the rhythmic steps. The dance follows the classical text of Hastha Lakshanadeepika, which has elaborate description of mudras.

The repertoire sequence of Mohiniyattam is similar to that of Bharatanatyam, and contains seven items that are performed to a structure described in classical dance texts: Cholkettu (invocation, but starts with offering reverence to a goddess Bhagavati and ends with a prayer to Shiva), Jatisvaram or more precisely *Swarajeti*, Varnam, Padam, Tillana, Shlokam and Saptam.

The costume includes white sari embroidered with bright golden brocade (known as kasavu) at the edges. The jewellery worn is in gold colour and the hair is tied with big bun surrounded with white flowers.

Among the present day artists Kalamandalam Sathyabhama, Kalamandalam Kshemavathi, Bharathi Sivaji, Kanak Rele, Sunanda Nair etc. are well known artists.

The accompaniments for Mohiniyattam are Vocal, Veena, Venu, Maddalam and Idakka.

KATHAK:

This dance form traces its origins to the nomadic bards of ancient northern India, known as Kathakars or storytellers. Its form today contains traces of temple and ritual dances, and the influence of the bhakti movement. From the 16th century it absorbed certain features of Persian dance and Central Asian dance which were imported by the royal courts of the Mughal era. The name Kathak is derived from the Sanskrit word *katha* meaning story.

There are three major schools or gharana of Kathak from which performers today generally draw their lineage: the gharanas of Jaipur, born in the courts of the Kachwaha Rajput kings, Lucknow gharana, born in the Nawab of Oudh and Varanasi gharana, born in Varanasi. There is also a less prominent (and later) Raigarh gharana which amalgamated technique from all three preceding gharanas but became famous for its own distinctive compositions.

The nritta structure of a Kathak performance begins from slow to fast pace, ending with a dramatic climax. The bols are borrowed from tabla (e.g. *dha, ge, na,* 'ti' 'na' 'ka' 'dhi na') or can be a dance variety (*ta, thei, tat, ta ta, tigda, digdig, tram theyi* and so on). The dancer recites these bols on stage during a performance.

The nritya or abhinaya pieces are performed to a bhajan, thumri, ghazal and bhaav bhataana. Even while seated, the abhinaya is done to single line many times. Shambhu Maharaj is claimed to have interpreted a single line in many different ways for hours. All the Maharaj family (Acchan Maharaj, Lachhu Maharaj, Shambhu Maharaj and Achhan Maharaj's son Birju Maharaj) have found much fame for the naturalness and innovativeness of their abhinaya.

Spins or chakkars are a prominent feature in kathak.

Extra Information: – (During the bhakthi movement kathak imbibed a lot of Krishna-radha stories in its dance form. Later during the mughal empire it imbibed the court style and the traditional form started withering away, only to be adopted with court entertainment. The emphasize was on the flamboyant and elaborate rhythmic footwork where the dancers wore as many as 150 ankle bells on each leg. It was also during this period that the signature 'chakkars' (spins) of Kathak were introduced, possibly influenced by the so-called whirling dervishes of Persian dancers.)

Lucknow Gharana: The Lucknow Gharana of Kathak dance came into existence mainly in the court of Nawab Wajid Ali Shah. The Lucknow style is characterized by graceful movements, elegance and natural poise with dance. Abhinaya is important in this style. Pandit Birju Maharaj is considered the chief representative of this gharana.

Jaipur Gharana: The *Jaipur Gharana* developed in the courts of the Kachchwaha kings of Jaipur in Rajasthan. Importance is placed on the more technical aspects of dance, such as complex and powerful footwork, multiple spins, and complicated compositions in different talas. Some of the famous dancers are Kundenlal Gangani, Sunderlal Gangani, Durga lal and presently Rajendra Gangani and Pratishtha Sharma.

Benaras/Varanasi Gharana: The *Benares Gharana* was developed by Janakiprasad. It is characterized by the exclusive use of the *natwari* or dance *bols*, which are different from the tabla and the pakhawaj *bols*.

Ghunghru are the small bells the dancer ties around his or her ankles. The usual number of bells is 100 on each ankle.

Traditional costume sometimes consists of a sari. However, more commonly, the costume is a *lehenga-choli* combination, with an optional *odhni* or veil. Mughal costume for women consists of an *angarkha* on the upper body. The design is akin to a chudidaar kameez, but is somewhat tighter fitting above the waist, and the 'skirt' portion explicitly cut on the round to enhance the flare of the lower half during spins.

The traditional costume for men is to be bare-chested. Below the waist is the dhoti, usually tied in the Bengal style. The Mughal costume is kurta churidar. The kurta can be a simple one, Men may also wear an *angarkha*.

The repertoire of Kathak begins with a Vandana, Thaat, Aamad, Salaami, Kavitt, Paran, Parmelu, Gat, Lari, Tihai and Toda.

SATTRIYA:

In the year 2000, the Sattriya dances of Assam received recognition as one of the eight classical dance forms of India. Sattriya has remained a living tradition since its creation by the founder of Vaishnavism in Assam, the great saint Srimanta Sankardev, in 15th century. Srimanta Sankardev and Madhavdev created Sattriya Nritya as an accompaniment to the Ankia Naat which were usually performed in the sattras, monasteries. As the tradition developed and grew within the sattras, the dance form came to be known as Sattriya Nritya.

Sattriya Nritya is divided into many aspects: Apsara Nritya, BeharNritya, ChaliNritya, DasavataraNritya.

Sattriya has two distinctly separate streams – the Bhaona-dependant repertoire starting from the Gayan-Bhayanar Nach to the Kharmanar Nach, secondly the dance numbers which are independent, such as Chali, Rajagharia Chali, Jhumura, Nadu Bhangi etc. Among them the Chali is characterized by gracefulness and elegance, while the Jhumura is marked by vigor and majestic beauty.

Sattriya Nritya follows the treaties Natyasastra, Abhinaya Darpana and Sangit Ratnakaar.

Sattriya Nritya is accompanied by musical compositions called borgeets which are based on classical ragas. The instruments that accompany a traditional performance are khols (drums), taals (cymbols) and the flute. Other instruments like the violin and the harmonium have been recent additions.

The costumes are usually made of pat – a silk produced in Assam which is derived from the mulberry plant. There are two types of costumes: the male costume comprising the dhoti and chadar and the female costume comprising the ghuri and chadar. The waist cloth which is known as the kanchi is worn by both the male and female dancers. The ornaments, too, are based on traditional Assamese design.

The jewelleries are made in a unique technique in *Kesa Sun* (raw gold). Female dancers wear white flowers in the hair.

Some of the leading exponents of Sattriya are Bapuram Barbayan Atai, Maniram Dutta Muktiyar Barbayan, Gahan Chandra Goswami, Jibeshwar Goswami, Lalit Chandra Nath Ojha.

MANIPURI:

Manipuri originates from Manipur, a state in north-eastern India on the border with Burma. The cult of Radha and Krishna, particularly the raslila, is central to its themes and the dances incorporate the characteristic cymbals (kartal or manjira) and double-headed drum (pung or Manipuri mrdanga) of sankirtan into the visual performance. Manipuri is unique among the classical Indian dances as the instrumentation is a central part of the dance, rather than as a side accompaniment. It is even often referred to as "sankirtan". The term Manipuri actually covers a number of dance forms from the region. The most important being the Ras Lila and the Pung Cholom.

There are a number of forms in Manipuri. These are the Ras Lila, the Pung Cholom, Nupa Cholom, Thoibi and many others.

Manipuri dance is purely religious and its aim is a spiritual experience. Manipuri dancers do not wear ankle bells to accentuate the beats tapped out by the feet, in contrast with other Indian dance forms, and the dancers' feet never strike the ground hard. Movements of the body and feet and facial expressions in Manipuri dance are subtle and aim at devotion and grace.

Maharaja Bhagyachandra (1759–1798 CE) of Manipur codified the style. Manipur became famous through the efforts of Rabindranath Tagore.

The lyrics used in Manipuri are usually from the classical poetry of Jayadeva, Vidyapati, Chandidas,Govindadas and may be in Sanskrit, Maithili, Brij Bhasha. Guru Naba Kumar, Guru Bipin Singh, Darshana Jhaveri are some of the prominent exponents of this classical dance form.

<u>COMPENDIUM</u>

BHARATANATYAM

CHARACTERISTICS	BHARATANATYAM
STATE	Tamil Nadu
REPERTOIRE/ MARGAM	allarippu, jathiswaram, shabdam, varnam, padam, thillana
IMPORTANT TEXT	Natya Sastra and Abhinaya Darpana
JEWELLERY	Temple Jewellry – salangai, waist band (daabu) bangles, chain, necklace, jumki, nethi chuti (head tikka), surya chandran – thalai samaan.
COSTUME	Kanchipuram silk sarees stitched in bharanatyam pant or skirt type of costume and Men wear dhoti and angavastra.
MUSIC AND INSTRUMENTS	Carnatic classical music. Instruments: Violin, mridangam, veena, nattuvangam, flute
PIONEERS	The Tanjore Quartet – Chinnaiah, Ponnaiah, Shivananda and Vadivelu
FAMOUS ARTISTS AND GURUS	Balasaraswathi, Padma Subramanyam, C V Chandrasekhar, Adyar K Lakshman, Saroja Vaidyanathan, U S Krishna Rao

KUCHIPUDI

CHARACTERISTICS	KUCHIPUDI
STATE	Andhra Pradesh and Telangana
REPERTOIRE/ MARGAM	Ganesh Vandana, Jatiswaram, Shabdam, Pravesha daru, Kalaapam, Padam, Tarangam
IMPORTANT TEXT	Abhinaya Darpana, Bharatanarva and Natya Sastra
JEWELLERY	Temple Jewellry – Gajjalu, waist band (odiyanam) bangles, chain, necklace, Kammalu (rings), paapita billa (head tikka), surya chandra
COSTUME	Silk saree stitched in pant or skirt costume. Men wear dhoti and Angavastra.
MUSIC AND INSTRUMENTS	Carnatic classical music. Instruments: Violin, mridangam, veena, nattuvangam, flute
PIONEERS	Sidhendra Yogi.
FAMOUS ARTISTS AND GURUS	Vedantam Lakshminarayana Sastri, Vempati Venkatanarayana Sastri and Chinta Venkataramayya, Vempati Chinna Satyam, C.R. Acharyalu, and Dr. Nataraja Ramakrishna, Raja Radha Reddy, Vyjayanthi Kashi.

ORISSI

CHARACTERISTICS	ORISSI
STATE	Odisha
REPERTOIRE/ MARGAM	Mangalacharan, Battu Nritya, Pallavi, Abhinaya, Moksha nritta.
IMPORTANT TEXT	Abhinaya Chandrika and Natya Sastra
JEWELLERY	Gold Jewellery – Waist band, bangles, chains, head tikka and white flowers around the huge bun on the hair
COSTUME	Kasavu Saree – White or half white with gold base.
MUSIC AND INSTRUMENTS	Odissi Music – Pakhawaj, Flute, Manjira, Sitar.
PIONEERS	Kavichandra Kalicharan Pattanayak
FAMOUS ARTISTS AND GURUS	Kelucharan Mohapatra, Pankaj Charan Das, Shoren Lowen, Mayadhar Raut, Ranjana Gauhar

MOHINIATTAM

CHARACTERISTICS	MOHINIATTAM
STATE	Kerala
REPERTOIRE/ MARGAM	Cholkattu, Swarajeti, Padavarnam, Padam, Thillana, Slokam, Saptam.
IMPORTANT TEXT	Hasta Lakshana Deepika and Natya Sastra

JEWELLERY	Gold
COSTUME	Kasavu saree
MUSIC AND INSTRUMENTS	Carnatic Music in Sopana style. Veena, Venu, Maddalam, Idakka
PIONEERS	Swathi Tirunal, Vadivelu, Vallathol, Kalyani Kutti amma
FAMOUS ARTISTS AND GURUS	Kalamandalam Sathyabhama, Kanak Rele, Sunanda Nair

KATHAKALI

CHARACTERISTICS	KATHAKALI
STATE	Kerala
REPERTOIRE/ MARGAM	Nalacharitam, Duryodhana Vadam, Kalyana sougandhikam, Poothana Vadam etc
IMPORTANT TEXT	Natya Sastra
JEWELLERY	Paccha, Dhadi, Minukku, Kari
COSTUME	Cotton huge skirt round in shape. Head gear, face mask.
MUSIC AND INSTRUMENTS	Sopanam style. Chenda, Maddalam, Idakka, cymbols
PIONEERS	Vallathol Narayana Menon
FAMOUS ARTISTS AND GURUS	Kalamandalam Ramankutty Nair, Kalamandalam Gopi, Chemencheri Kunhiraman Nair

SATTRIYA

CHARACTERISTICS	SATRIYA
STATE	Assam
REPERTOIRE/ MARGAM	Apsara Nritya, Behar Nritya, Jhumara, Nadu Bangi, Sutradhara
IMPORTANT TEXT	Abhinaya Darpana, Sangita Ratnakara, Natya Sastra
JEWELLERY	Kesa Sun – Assamese Traditional Jewellery. Kopali, Muthi and Gam Kharu, Mata Moni etc.
COSTUME	Paat silk – with local motifs. Women wear – Guri, Chadar and Kanchi. Men wear – Dhoti, chadar and paguri.
MUSIC AND INSTRUMENTS	Borgeets on classical ragas. Khols, cymbals, Flute, Violin, Harmonium
PIONEERS	Srimanta Shankardev and Madhavdev
FAMOUS ARTISTS AND GURUS	Baburam Barbayan Atai, Gahan Chandra Goswami, lalit Chadra Nath Ojha

KATHAK

CHARACTERISTICS	Kathak
STATE	North India
REPERTOIRE/ MARGAM	Vandana, Thaat, Aamad, Salaami, Kavitt, Paran, Parmelu, Gat, Lari, Tihai and Toda.

IMPORTANT TEXT	Natya Sastra
JEWELLERY	Stones with gold covering
COSTUME	Angarekha, gagra skrit, salwar kameez. Dhoti or angharekha for men.
MUSIC AND INSTRUMENTS	Hindustani. Pakhawaj, dolak, table, sitar.
PIONEERS	Lachu and Achan Maharaj, Gangani
FAMOUS ARTISTS AND GURUS	Birju Maharaj, Rajendra Prasad Gangani, Nirupama Rajendra, Aditi Mangaldas.

MANIPURI

CHARACTERISTICS	Manipuri
STATE	Manipur
REPERTOIRE/ MARGAM	Ras Lila, the Pung Cholom, Nupa Cholom, Thoibi
IMPORTANT TEXT	Natya Sastra
JEWELLERY	Stones with gold covering
COSTUME	Drum shaped skirt, dhuppata on head and a beaded and stone blouse. Dhoti kurta for men.
MUSIC AND INSTRUMENTS	Manipuri sangeet, Hindustani. Pakhawaj, dolak, table, sitar.
PIONEERS	Guru Bhagyachandra
FAMOUS ARTISTS AND GURUS	Guru Naba Kumar, Guru Bipin Singh, Darshana Jhaveri

DEFINITIONS OF DANCE-TERMS

PATRA: (Qualifications) The dancer should posses a good structure should be young with rounded breasts, experienced, charming, well versed in rhythmic skills, in movements of the body, with large well shaped eyes, able to follow the song, instrument and rhythm, good sense of dressing, sparkling face, not too stout nor too thin, not too tall nor too short, intelligent and multi-talented.

APATRA: (disqualifications): A women with scanty hair, thick lips, pendent breasts, very fat or very tall, very thin or stout, hunch back are not suitable for dance.

SABHA: The audience which is the wishing tree (kalpa vruksha) shines with the Vedas as its branches, the sastras as its flowers and the scholors as the bees adoring it. This is the description given by Nandikeshwara in Abhinaya Darpana. Sabha is compared to Kalpa-vruksha.

PATRA – ANTHAH PRANAS: (inner life of the danseuse) Inner aspects of the life of a danseuse should be without any sins, natya rekha (purity of form). The different techniques of bramari, the various glances of eyes, perfect composure and with ease and intelligence the dancer should be deeply devoted to her act, possess good speech and song. These elaborate and detailed rules were to be taken consideration by all artists and spectators of dance, drama and music to perfect the art forms.

PATRA-BAHIRPRANA: (outer life of the danseuse) The drum (mridangam), the sweet sounding cymbols, the drone, flute, veena, bells and the singer of melodious tone are the outer life of a dancer.

KINKINI: (bells) The bells should be made of bronze, copper or silver. They should posses a melodious tone and be of pleasing shape and have the stars as their presiding deity. They should be strong together on a black thread with a knot between each. For the performance, the dancer may use either a hundred or two hundred on each of her feet. Alternatively a hundred on the right and two hundred on the left foot may also be used.

JATHI: This is a combination of 2 or more adavus with complicated footwork and hand movements always ending with a Mukthaya. This will generally be in three speeds. So jathi is Korvai + Mukthaya.

MUKTHAYI: Mukthayi is presented before the starting (which is mostly not danced) and at the finishing of dance. It is a movement ending a group of movements and is usually repeated thrice. Eg: tha ding gina thom. The end of a Jathi is a mukthayi.

THEERMANA:

Nattuvanar perception: The set of technical utterances or bols, set to define a chain of adavus is called theermanam. This can be in any jaathi and in any thala. The length of the theermanam is not restricted. The syllables of the cymbals define a particular theermana for dancing. In other words, the sound that is heard from the cymbols becomes a theermana when danced.

Mridangist perception: Theermanam is a Mukthayi which is played at the end or beginning of the jathi.

Dancer perception: The jathi which is performed is also a called theermanam.

KORVAI: The word Korvai means to compile, join or thread together. Korvais are adavus when set to a particular Talam (Rhythm) and Kalam (speed) and usually concludes with a Theermanam. Jatiswaram and Tillana are pure dance pieces, where many such korvais are joined together.

NAATYAKRAMA: Rules of Dance:

A sound thinking should be done before beginning an auspicious dance program. Salutations should be offered at the very beginning. Nandikeshwara guides dancers to perfection with the following techniques: a dancer must behold music in throat, enact meaning to the lyrics through hand gestures and feeling through the eyes and rhythm in the feet.

SLOKA: *Kantena Lambayet gitam, hastena artham pradarshayet |*
Chakshurbhyam darshayet bhaavam, paadabhyaam taalam acharet | |

A dancer must have her eyes following hands, consciemce following glance, expression following conscience and aesthetic element of emotions (rasa) following the expression.

SLOKA: *Yatho hasta tatho dhrishtih yatho dhrishtih tatho manah |*
Yatho manah tatho bhaavah yatho bhaava tatho rasah | |

MAATRA: Matra is a beat, the smallest rhythmic sub-unit of a tala – the musical meter. The significance of beats depends on their occurrence in a cycle. However, the value of the beats may be stretched or contracted depending on various factors.

AVARTANA: The avaratana is the cycle of thala in Music. It is composed of measures (vibhaga) which are in turn composed of beats (matra). Indian musicians typically will not mix the measures. For instance aadi is two measures of four-beats, four-beats, however the overall 8 beat pattern may not be altered. Avartans may be of any number of beats, depending on the jaathi.

The most common numbers are 16, 14, 12, 10, 8, 7, and 6. Most of the music played in India today is in one of these numbers. The rhythmic cycle of a particular thala is a avaratana.

ANGA/VIBHAAGA: The angas are constituent units of a thala. For example the famous adi tala takes the following angas: 1 laghu and 2 dhrutams. The adi thala is technically called chatusra jaathi triputa thala as the laghu contains four beats. The angas are of six types, they are called Shadangas. They are:

1. Laghu
2. Dhrutam
3. Anudhrutam
4. Guru
5. Kaakapaadam
6. Plutam

PADA BHEDAS:

Vakshyate padabhedanam lakshnam purwasammatam | |
Mandalaotplavane chaiva bhramari padacharika |
chaturdha padabhedah suh tesham lakshana – muchyate | |

There are four types of movements of feet as described by the ancient scholars. They are 1. Mandala, 2. Utplavana, 3. Bhramaris and 4. Padacharika.

MANDALA BHEDAS: (half sitting positions)

STHANAKA BHEDAS: (Standing positions)

UTPLAVANA BHEDAS: (jumping)

BHARAMARI BHEDAS: (circling)

CHARI BHEDAS: (movements)

CHAPTER 03

FAMOUS COMPOSERS AND DANCE GURUS

KALYANI KUTTI AMMA (1915 – 1999):

The origin of Mohiniattam has been traced to dasiattam, developed by devadasis of kerela temple in the past. Kalyani Kutti amma and her daughter Sri devi did a lot of research in chera, chola and pandiyan period and traced it back to dasi attam, thevidhichi attam and sadi attam.

She read books on history, visited temples where dance was performed and even interviewed the descendants of devadasi. She reformed the recital of mohiniattam with 7 different sets of items choreographed charis and adavus and grouped under 4 types: Thaganam, Jaganam, Dhaganam and Samishram and reconsturcted Sapatam. She composed Sollukattu, Jathiswaram, Varnam, Padam, Thillana, Slokam in malayalam. She introduced Navarasa to songs in malayalam and composed slokas, kritis and 80 stanzas of technique of mohiniattam. She conducted several workshops and seminars. She preached that every dancer should know "Balarama Bharata" written by Karthikeyan Thirunal Verma. She wrote two books in Malyalam and four full fledged ballets (dance drama). She also acted in movies, some of her movies are "aswavittu", "gandharva kshetram", "rendu mukangal". She was a recipient of Kavithri-Vallathol, SNA fellowship, Kerela SNA fellowship, Kerela Sahitya Academy

Awards. She passed away in the year 1999 at the age of 84. Today her daughter Sri Devi and her daughters run the institute of teaching dance.

JETTI TAYAMMA:

Jetti Tayamma is the daughter of a wrestler named Dasappa, engaged during the Mummadi Krishnaraja Wodeyar. She learnt dance and sanskrit from Subbrayappa and Kanchinattuva, Alankara and abhinaya from Shringeri Subramanya Shastry. She was a very intelligent girl and shined as a gem from young age in the court of Mysore. She became the main dancer at the court of Chamaraja and krishnaraja Wodeyar. Her father was a learned person and he sang very well especially the kshetrayya padams. When she was 6 years, she showed interest in Dance, music. After learning Nritta part of dance she took further training in abhinay from Asthana Vidwan Kavishwara Giriyappa, Telugu javali and padam from Chandrasekhara Shastry, Kannada songs and jaavali from Kavi basappa Shastry, who is also known as Abhinava Kalidasa. She was a palace dancer at the age of 15 and was a great favourite for all vidwans. Since she knew sanskrit very well, she used to dance to Amaru, Krishna Karnamrutham, Gita Govindam and Kalidasa's work with ease. She introduced choornika in dance. She knew many javali and padams both in telugu and kannasa and later composed javalis while performing. Sangeeta Shastra Visharad Asthana Vidwan Mysore Vasudevacharya presented her with a Vamana stotra in raagamalika. During the time of Chamaraja Wodeyar, Jetti Tayamma gave up dancing due to dissatisfaction with the change of policies by the management. Nevertheless she continued to give performance of abhinaya at her residence which gathered many audience including scholars who sat engrossed by her poetic rendition of songs.

Jetti Tayamma also learnt Hindusthani style of music and dance from artists visiting the palace and rendered thumris to the accompaniment of Sarangi and tabla. She laid emphasis on abhinaya and believed that Rasa-Abhinaya was the soul of dance. She maintained rigid routine of practice and even at the age of 80 she continued to do so. In 1945, she was conferred "Natya Saraswathi" title by Dr Radhakrishnan in Maharaja College, Mysore. She passed away in November 1947, she left behind a great tradition of Bharatanatyam which is being maintained by her disciples. One her famous disciple is K.Venkatalakshamma.

MEENAKSHI SUNDARAM PILLAI (1869-1954):

The Pandanallur style of Bharatanatyam was popularised by Meenakshi Sundaram Pillai, Muthukumar Pillai, Kittappa Pillai and Subbarayya Pillai. He is a descendant of the Tanjore Quartet. He was a dance Guru who lived in the village of Pandanallur, which is in Tamil Nadu. He learnt under Tanjore Quartet and later became the son-in-law of Shivanandam. Meenakshisundaram Pillai was said to have been trained by his uncle Kumarasamy Nattuvanar. He trained several famous Bharatanatyam dancers including devadasis such as Pandanallur Jayalakshmi, Thangachi Ammal, Sabaranjitam, as well as people from other castes such as Mrinalini Sarabhai, Rukmini Devi, Tara Chaudhri and others. The Pandanallur style has a reputation for its emphasis on linear geometry in adavu technique and for intensity and under statement in abhinaya.

The Pandanallur style is renowned for its masterpieces in choreography: some of the main gems in its repertoire are the Nine or Ten Tanjore Quartet *pada-varnams* (Sakiye, Sami Ninne,

Mohamana, Danike, Adimogam, Yemaguva, Sami Nee Ramanave, Sarasijanaba) for which Meenakshi Sundaram Pillai composed the choreography: both dramatic choreography which he called simply "hands" as well as the *adavu* choreography for the *swara* passages.

Also, part of their heritage are the valuable jatiswarams (in *ragams Vasantha, saveri, chakravakam, kalyani, bhairavi)* which are miniature masterpieces of elegant abstract adavu choreography.

Pandanallur style also gives a lot of importance to Abhinaya, Moreover stamping the foot hard against the floor is discouraged in this style. Instead slow movements are used to make the salangai give out a lot of noise.

He was the first teacher at kalakshetra, Chennai.

VENKATALAKSHMAMMA:

Classical imagery was always an allegory, an art for the dancers – not a trade, Dr K Venkatalakshmamma exemplified this spirit till her final adieu not only by word but also deed. She was a person with sharp intellect, ready wit and liveliness.

Born in a Banjara family, in Kadur District, Karanataka, she had no background in art. She had to go through lot of hardships, a quagmire of obstacles, prejudices. At the tender age of 8, she came to Mysore. Her only mission was to study under the quintessential guidance of Natya Saraswathi Jetti Tayamma. Jetti Tayamma, a purist found unexplored talent in Venkatalakshmamma. She learnt music from Dr. B. Devendrappa and C Rama Rao, Sanskrit from Vidwan Devothama lois. She had the honour to perform dance recitals with her guru. She became Asthana Vidushi in the court of Krishnaraja Wodeyar and Chamaraja Wodeyar, the last of Wodeyar dynasty for over

40 years. She has contributed immensely to the field of dance. She has trained a host of dancers both in India and Abroad. She was a faculty and also principal in many institutions, including the faculty of dance in University of Mysore, Nupura school of Bharatanatyam, Bangalore.

She is a recipient of National Academy Award, Sangeeta kala Ratna, Padma Bhushan, State regional Academy Award. Venkatalakshmamma was a rigid teacher, perfectionist and fastidious dancer.

KOLARA PUTTAPPA:

Vidvan Kolara puttappa is one of the greatest exponents of Bharatanatyam. He learnt nattuvangam under Vidvan Kolara Kittappa. His disciples are U S Krishnarao and U K Chandrabhagadevi. He was a very great perso at heart and generous artist.

N GUNDAPPA:

Disciple of Kolara Kittappa. He has composed jathiswara, swarajathi and jaavali. His disciples are V S Koushik and H R Keshavamurthy. He is a teacher from the Mysuru style of dancing. A great dance teacher, nattuvanar and popular artist.

CHOKKALINGA PILLAI:

Disciple of Pandanallur Meenakshi Sundaram Pillai.

He worked in Kalakshetra. He also worked as principal of Indian Institute of Fine Arts.

His son was Subbraya Pillai.

Disciples are Mrinalini Sarabhai, Indrani Rehman.

V RAMAIAH PILLAI:

Vazhuvoor Ramaiah pillai was a very famous nattuvanar. His style is Vazhuvoor style. He lived in the court of King Sharabhoji maharaj II. His son was Samaraj continued his style for 40 years. His prime disciple was Kumari Kamala Lakshman. Lalitha-padmini-ragini, padma Subrahmanyam, vyjayanthi mala are notable some of his disciples. He implemented Rama Natak kriti, Thyagaraja swamy kritis, Bharathiyar songs, Kutralak Kuravanji songs in Bharatanatyam through his instructions. During the time that the British had banned Bharathiyar's songs, Vazhuvoor made these songs performed by his students in stage plays, thereby encouraging the support of Indian Independence. Swamimalai Raja Rathnam Pillai is the son of Ramaiah Pillai, who is also a very notable artist in the vuzhuvur style.

PUTTADEVAMMA: Great dancer in the mysuru court.

TANJORE BROTHERS:

The four brothers who uplifted dance and music in temples were Chinnaiah, Ponnaih, Shivananda and Vadivelu. They were celebrated for their knowledge of dance and music. Ponnaiah and Shivananda were attached to the Brihadheeswara temple of Tanjore during the region of Maharaja Sharobji. Chinnaiah was the official teacher in the court of Maharaja Krishna rajendra Wodeyar. Vadivelu was appointed as the musician in Tanjore at the court of Maharaja Swathi Thirunal.

CHINNAIAH: (1802):

He is the eldest of all the four brothers who was attached to the Mysore palace as an artist during the period of maharaja Chamaraya Wodeyar II. He composed many padavarnams, thillanas, padams in praise of Goddess Chamundeshwari. He also composed some Padavarnamas in the name of the Maharaja as a gesture of gratitude to the Maharaja Chamaraja Wodeyar under whose protection he lived.

PONNAIAH: (1804):

Chinnaiah younger brother Ponnaiah thought of bringing dance on with music so that it could be performed always at any place just as the music has the beginner's lessons like sarali, janta, alankara, varnams etc. Ponnaiah Pillai catagorised the adavus varieties into ten groups Ponnaiah Pillai arranged the following system: Allarippu, Jathiswaram, Shabdham, Varnam etc. These items were composed in different ragas and thalas. The padavarnam and swarajathi composed by Ponnaiah Pillai were full of Nayaka and Nayaki bhavas. Guru Muthuswamy Deekshitar was very much impressed by their work and gave a title "Sangeeta Sahitya Bharata Shreshta" through the maharaja.

It is also said that once when his brother was sick Ponnaiah composed a a song on Brihadambika in Shanakarabharanam raga and sang it with great devotion. After this, his brother got cured of his ailment.

The training for Bharatanatyam took 7 years under the direction of Nattuvanars.

SHIVANANDAM: (1808):

Shivanandam is the younger brother to Chinnaiah and Ponnaiah. He gets the credit of making dance art suitable to be presented at the temples by comprising songs with Bhakthi bhavas. His compositions include deepaaradhana, thala jathi, shoda upachara and flag hoisting, nava sandhi nritya (sky and sun), navagraha pooja and kouthuvams. He has composed jathis for processions of Lord Nataraja as per the mela thala played during that time. For this procession he establised the dancing in the temples as prepared by his elder brother Ponnaiah. Shivananda and maharaja of Tanjore were very close friends. Shivananda had a very good voice and could sing at 4 1/2 pitch. He composed many Swarajathis, varnamas, padamvarnam in praise of Gods and kings of Tanjore. He took all the artists to various places and made them sing and dance to popularise the fine arts. He was also a good a painter. He used to paint sketches and explain to his students through sketching. Shivananda proved that dance could be performed not only by ladies but also by gents.

It was he who introduced dance during temple festicals and this system is still continued. The credit of constructing the dance hall for this purpose also goes to Shivananda. He was a very great devotee of lord shiva and offered his very navaratna mala to lord shiva at Bruhadheeshwara on shivaratri day.

VADIVELU: (1810):

Vadivelu is the youngest of the four brothers. He paid special attention to music connected with dance. He practised with great devotion and became an outstanding musician and composer.

Once a foreigner who was a violin exponent came to Tanjore palace to perform. Vadivelu was very much pleased with his performance and asked him (a christian father) to stay in the palace. The chritian father presented violin instrument to Vadivelu and also taught him to play western music on violin. Vadivelu then innovated the idea of playing carnatic music on violin and was the first person to play carnatic music on violin.

The foreign priest was very much pleased with Vadivelu's innovation and so also the Maharaja, scholors and musicians.

During that period, the Travancore Maharaja Swathi Tirunal was highly respected and regarded as an exponent of all arts. Tanjore Maharaja heard about the artistic talents of the four brothers and decided to invite them to his palace.

Vadivelu's rendition on violin please the maharaja very much and he presented him with an ivory violin. Vadivelu became very close to Swathi Tirunal Maharaja and helped him in composing many songs also mohiniattam dance. Vadivelu stayed back with Swathi Tirunal.

Saint Thyagaraja also had high regards for the 4 brothers. Ponnaiah passed at the age of 60, Shivananda at the age of 55, Vadivelu at 53, Chinnaiah passed away within a short period of Vadivelu's death. Maharaja Swathi Tirunal attained moksha shortly after that.

CHAPTER 04

KNOWLEDGE OF MUSICAL INSTRUMENTS AND MUSIC

The origins of Indian classical music can be found in the Vedas. Music was derived from Sama veda and its hymns could be sung as Samagana. It divides the octave into the 7 basic notes which are called Svara. They are *Sa Re Ga Ma Pa Dha Ni*. Bharat's Natyashastra was the first treatise laying down fundamental principles of dance, music, and drama. The performance is based on Raga and Thala.

There are two types of music, Hindustani and Carnatic music. Instruments typically used in Hindustani music includethe sitar, sarod, surbahar, veena, tanpura, bansuri, shehnai, sarangi, violin, santoor, pakhavaj and tabla. Instruments typically used in Carnatic music include venu, gottuvadyam, harmonium, veena, mridangam, kanjira, ghatam and violin.

The Instruments are mainly divided into 4 kinds – thatha, sushira, avanadha and Ghana.

- **Thatha** – String instruments are known as Thatha. Eg – Veena, Sitar, Violin, Sarod, Tambura, Santoor.

- **Sushira** – Wind instruments are known as Sushira. Eg – flute, Nadhaswaram, shehnai, harmonium, clarionet.

- **Avanadha** – Percussion instruments made of animal skin is known as Avanadha. Eg – Mridanga, tabla, Dolak,

Pakhavaj, Damru, maddal, pung, Kanjira, tavil, udukkai, idakka.

- **Ghana** – Percussion instruments made of metal, wood or earthern ware is known as Ghana. Eg – bells, ghatam, cymbals, khartal, thattukazhi mannai, chimpta, chengila, jal tarang.

RAAGA: There are totally 72 different ragas in Indian classical music. They are called the Janaka ragas or Melakarta. There are various Janya ragas born from these janaka which provides us with variety of ragas. The Swaras are

Sa – Shadja
Ri – Rishabha
Ga – Gandhara
Ma – Madhyama
Pa – Panchama
Da – Dhaivatha
Ni – Nishadha.

These swaras have Arohana – the ascending order and Avorahana – the decending order. The combination of these swaras in aroha and avaroha makes a unique raga.

THALA: Thala or rhythmic cycle in Indian music is of vital importance. 7 main thala and 5 Jaathi for each thala which will give us 35 thalas. So, there are 35 thalas in total. *(extra information: – when combined with 5 nadais, it will give a total of 175 thalas altogether)* Thala is indicated by Shashabdha and Nishabdha kriye. Vishranthi after thala kriye is called Laya. There are three kinds of layas (speed) namely Vilambha (slow), Madhyama (Faster), Dhrutha (Fast) which is called Thrikala. The completion of a thala is called Avartha.

The seven main thalas or Sapta thalas and the 5 jaathis and their symbols are in the below table:

NAME	SYMBOL	T – 3	C – 4	K-5	M-7	S-9
Dhruva	1011	11	14	17	23	29
Matya	101	8	10	12	16	20
Jumpa	1U0	6	7	8	10	12
Triputa	100	7	8	9	11	13
Roopaka	o1	5	6	7	9	11
Ata	1100	10	12	14	18	22
Eka	1	3	4	5	7	9

T – Tisra, C – Chatusra, K – Khanda, M – Misra, S – Sankeerna

7 * 5 = 35 Thalas

To show the thala, few actions are made such as throwing and beating, waving of the hands, counting fingers etc with the help of these actions the thala angas are shown. This is called kriya/ kriye.

The parts or angas of thala are divided into three main components. They are Druta, Lagu and Anudruta. There are others which Guru, Kaakapaadam and plutam.

- Druta – **Symbol – 0.** The measurement of thala with one beat (dhruvaka) and waving it over (Visarjitha) is called druta. This uses two kriye.

- Lagu – **Symbol – 1.** The measurement of thala beginning with one beat (Dhruvaka) and counting of the fingers starting with little finger (Vikshipta) is called lagu. This uses two kriye.The number of counting changes according to the Jaathi/Gaathi.

- Anudruta – **Symbol – U.** The measurement of thala with one beat is called anudrutam. It occurs only in Jumpa thala. This uses one kriye.

- Guru – **Symbol – 8.** One beat and fall of fingers in clockwise direction, starting with index finger is guru.

- Plutam – **Symbol-8**

- Kaakapaadam – **Symbol – +**

The gaathis or Jaathis are five in number. They are:

- Tisra – This is a count of three. THA KI TA.

- Chaturasra – This is a count of four. THA KA DHI MI.

- Khanda – This is a count of five. THA KA THA KI TA.

- Misra – This is a count of seven. THA KA DHI MI THA KI TA.

- Sankeerna – This is a count of nine. THA KA DHI MI THA KA THA KI TA.

CHAPTER 05

DANCE SCULPTURES IN KARNATAKA

Dance and sculpture are two different art forms yet they are interlinked in social, cultural, historical and religious streams. These two art forms are developed and nurtured by temples in India. Sculptural representations of dance have preserved beautiful movements and striking moments of the ancient dance traditions. Both of them are used as vehicles to express human emotions and aesthetic achievement. Both the art forms have chosen human body as the means for their expression. Evoking rasa or rasotpatti in the minds of onlookers is the ultimate aim of a dancer and a sculptor.

The antiquity of Architecture of Karnataka can be traced to its southern Neolithic and early Iron Age. Its architecture ranges dramatically from majestic monolith, such as the Gomateshwara, to Hindu and Jain places of worship, ruins of ancient cities, palaces of different architectural hue. Mysore Kingdom (Wodeyar) rule has also given an architectural master structure.

Below is the list of temples where we can find architectural skills in Karnataka:

ARCHITECTURE	TEMPLES	SPECIALITY	TIME
Kadamba Architecture	Doddagaddavalli Hoyasala, Mahakuta temple in Hampi, Madhukeshwar in Banavasi	Kadamba Shikara	345-525
Dravidian Architecture	Gomateshwar, Shravanabelagola, Talakadu, Nanjangud, Sattur, Hangala		350-550
Badami Chalukya Architecture	Badami and Aihole temple	Rock hut halls, Surface structural monuments	5-8th century
Dravidian and Rashtrakutas	Pattadakal, Sanghameshwar, Papanatha, Navalinga, Galaganatha temple		7-8th century
Western Chalukya Architecture	Lakkundi, kashivishwanatha, Mahadeva, Siddesvara, Trikuteshwar Shiva temples.		11-12th century
Hoyasala Architecture	Somanathpur, Chennakeshava, Hoyasalawar, Melakote, Lakshminaraswamy temples	Stone works	10-11th century

ARCHITECTURE	TEMPLES	SPECIALITY	TIME
Vijayanagar Architecture	Hampi, Bhatkal, Sringeri, Ahobilam, Tirupathi, Virupaksha temples	Kalyana and vasantha mantapa and Rajagopura	13-16th century

Distinguished Art historians like Percy Brown, Kapila Vatsyayan place Karnataka high in the evolution and development of temple architecture and historical sculptures.

Hoyasala architecture: Dance has influenced Hoysala sculptures so deeply that even ordinary scenes like pulling out a thorn from the sole of the foot, writing a letter or applying a tilaka on the forehead are all portrayed in a dance-like attitude in these sculptures. The regional variations of dance form and musical instruments are very well represented throughout the Hoysala complex. The dancing icons, celestials and madanikas are chosen to decorate the inner and outer parts of the temple.

Vijayanagar architecture: The Vijayanagara rulers encouraged art and architecture to a large extent. Pillars of Virupaksha and Achyutaraya temples have some exquisite dance sculptures including both Marga and Deśī karana. The outer wall panels of Hazara Rama temple its known for its dance sculptures depicting Kolata, Holi dance sequences. The sculptures of Achyutaraya temple, Vijaya Vithala temple and Krishna temple have some rare and charming dance images and include different sthana, charis and karanas.

The Hoysala and Vijayanagara temples where we can find sculptures are:

1. Chennakeshava Temple, Belur,
2. Hoysaleshwara Temple, Halebidu,

3. Kedareshwara Temple, Halebidu,

4. Veeranarayana Temple, Belavadi,

5. Virupaksha Temple, Hampi,

6. Hazara Rama Temple, Hampi,

7. Krishna Temple, Hampi,

8. Achyutaraya Temple, Hampi,

9. Vijaya Vittala Temple, Hampi,

10. Mahanavami Dibba, Hampi.

Medieval period treatises such as Saṅgīta Ratnākara, Mānasollāsa, Nṛtta Ratnāvali, Saṅgīta Samayasāra, Lāsya Ranjana etc. have given elaborate description about deśī tradition. In Hoyasaleshwara temple in Halebidu, we find a dancing figure in slightly bent kati and kunchita swasthika accompanied by two musicians. In Chennakeshava temple we find "Shilabanjike". One of them is the beautiful and charming shilabhanjika, in ekapada sthana. *(Extra Information: – She seems to be busy adjusting her ear ring by looking at the mirror. The mood of vasaka sajjike has been captured by the sculptor through this graceful stance, with an emphasis on kati bending.)* We also find a paraavrtta pose in chennakeshava temple. We find male dancers in ratha chakra chaari in Vijaya Vittala Temple in Hampi. In Belur, Chennakeshava temple, there are Madanikas sculpture, which is very famous for their beauty. There is also a Nrutya Gannapa or Dancing Ganesha who is in Kutta mode (striking the ground with tip of the toe) in Halebidu.

GUPTA PERIOD:

The peace and prosperity in the Gupta Empire initiated a period known as the Golden Age of India because it was marked by extensive inventions and discoveries in science, technology, engineering, art, dialectic, literature, logic, mathematics, astronomy, religion, and philosophy.

Extra Information:-

- *Chandragupta II promoted the synthesis of science, art, philosophy, and religion in part.*

- *Strong trade relationships made the Gupta Empire an important cultural center and its Golden Age advancements influenced Burma, Sri Lanka, and Southeast Asia.*

- *Ayurvedic: A form of alternative medicine that was established in India.*

- *Navartna: Navaratna meaning the Nine Jewels, was a group of nine scholars in the court of Chandragupta II who contributed to many advancements in their academic fields*

- *Authors:*

  - *Dandin wrote the book 'Kavyadarsa' and 'Dasakumaracharita'.*

  - *Vasavadatta was written by Subhandhu.*

  - *Visakadatta was other renowned author of this period. He was the author of two dramas: Mudrarakshasa and Devichandraguptam.*

  - *The Panchatantra stories were composed by Vishnusarma during the Gupta period.*

  - *Sudraka was a renowned poet. He wrote his book Mrichchakatika.*

  - *Bharavi's Kritarjuniya is the story of discriminations between Arjuna and Siva.*

  - *The Buddhist author Amarasimha created Amarakosa.*

  - *The paintings of Ajantha mostly demonstrating the life of the Buddha was during this period.*

- *Science and Scholars: Scholars of this period include Varahamihira and Aryabhata; Aryabhata is believed to be the first to come up with the concept of zero and who postulated the theory that the Earth moves round the Sun. Aryabhata proposed that the earth is not flat, but is instead round and rotates about its own axis. He also may have discovered that the Moon and planets shine by reflected sunlight.*

- *The famous Sushruta Samhita, which is a Sanskrit redaction text on all of the major concepts of ayurvedic medicine with innovative chapters on surgery, dates to the Gupta period.*

- *The game of chess originated from this period, where its early form was called chaturanga.*

- *Kalidasa, who was a great playwright, wrote plays such as Shakuntala, which is said to have inspired German writer and stateman, Johann von Goethe centuries later, and marked the highest point of Sanskrit literature, which is also said to have belonged to this period.*

CHAPTER 06

ORIGIN OF DANCE – NATYOPATHI

(According to *Natya Sastra*)

"Pranamya Shirasa devo pithamaha Maheshwaro |
Natyasastra pravakshyami Brahmaana yadhudhahrutham | |"

'Bowing to pitamaha and Maheswara, I shall narrate the art of drama as taught to me by Lord Brahma'

In the days of yore, the high souled sages approached the master of Natya and requested him to narrate the origin of 5th Veda.ie. Natya Veda. This Natya Veda later came to be called "the Natya Sastra" or "the science of Dramatics". Bharata Muni, the author of Natya Sastra explained the Natya Veda in the following manner:

During the golden and silver age, people became addicted to sensual pleasure which led to greed and jealousy and finally brought sorrow to the people of 'Jambu dweepa'. Jambu dweepa was full of Gods, Dhanavas, Ghandharvas, Yakshyas, Nagas and Rakshas. The head of all Gods was Indra and he approached Bhagawan Brahma and requested Him to give them an object of diversion which should help both the intelligent and illiterates of the society. Hence it had to be both audible and visual in nature. This 5th veda was to be based on four existing Vedas and the itihasa (semi historical) stories leading to Dharma, Artha and Yashas. It would be a boon to humanity. It should also include the essence of all the Scriptures (Sastras), arts and crafts (shilpas) and serve as a guide to future generations. Brahma being the only one who mastered all the 4 vedas agreed to Indra's suggestion and started meditating to create Natya Veda. He took Recitation from the Rig Veda, Music from Sama Veda, Gestures and abhinaya from Yajur Veda and Rasa from Atharvana Veda.

Indra knew that the devas were highly sensual beings and he felt that Rishis were capable of preserving the Natya Veda. Hence Bharata Muni was summoned by Brahma asking him to put Natya Veda into practice with the help of his 100 sons. Thus began the training in Dramaturgy.

On the completion of training, Bharata Muni introduced 3 Vrittis (Styles). i.e. Bharati (speech and words), Sashavathi (movements with beauty) and Arabhati (vigorous) for the play production. When the play was presented before Brahma, he felt it was devoid of grace and hence he asked to add another Vritti – Kaisiki Vritti. But Bharata Muni had no ladies to perform this as the style required good Angaharas, postures, rasas and bhavas. He once again requested Brahma to give him female dancers. Brahma created the Apsaras who were well trained so Bharata could add Kaisiki Vritti in play production.

Thereafter Bharata Muni approached Brahma and requested him to suggest a platform to perform. Brahma told him about the Banner (Jarjara) festival which was a celebration in favour of Indra's victory over Dhanavas and Asuras.

Bharata Muni felt that the chosen festival was an ideal one for the production. The spectators who were present included the Dhaityas who came uninvited along with Dhanavas, Asuras, gandharvas etc. They enjoyed the play until the time where their defeat was shown. This episode made them furious as they did not wish to see their defeat on stage. They instigated Virupaksha, their leader to stop the play with obstacles. The Rakshas created a spell on actors who became still and speechless. Seeing this Indra was furious and he took his Banner staff to destroy all the Vignas. The actors extended their gratitude to Indra Deva and praised him for his deed. Then they renamed the banner (Dvaja) as Jarjara meaning shredding of evil force. This is the reason all art forms place the Jarjara on the right side of the stage to ward away all evil after the customary Purvaranga.

The Natya Veda that bhagawan Brahma devised is the mimicry of action and conduct of people which is rich in emotion. Drama will help a man to learn his mistakes by watching and improvising.

While presenting the play "Amrutha Mathana" Bharata invited Bhagawan Shiva to see the rehearsals and Shiva who saw the production was pleased and suggested the introduction of Pure dance in the Purvaranga. This dance had the beautiful use of Angaharas, Karanas along with the Asarita with Geeta and Maha Geeta, a combination of Pure dance and bhava. Shiva also helped in training the pure dance through one of his ganas by name Thandu and he, inturn taught Bharata Muni. Bharata Muni after taking training from Thandu named the style after him – The Thandava. Parvati trained Bana sura's daughter Usha in Lasya form and later Usha came down to Dwaraka and imparted the training to the Gopis. Hence the two major styles – The Thandava and Lasya emerged during Natyopathi.

Four types of vrittis were found by Brahma. The 4th vrittis which is called as Kaisiki (graceful movements & expressions) could not be done by the men. Hence Brahma created 24 Apsara for the use of Kaisiki.

Natya Veda was written by Bharata Muni in 36 chapters and 6000 verses which spoke about the rules of dance, drama and music in form of Natya Sastra. He also divided places into 4 zones – Avanti, Panchala, Dhakshin Natya and Odhra Magadi and asked the people to lay the precepts of Natya Veda to their regional values. Thus Natya Veda was created and installed in the regional dance-drama forms.

Extras:

Pravrittis and Vrittis which are more prevelant:

- *Avanti – west (kaisiki and sathvathi)*
- *Dhakshinatya – South (kaisiki)*
- *Panchali – North (Arabhati and sathvathi)*
- *Odra Magadi – East (Kaisiki and bharathi)*

According to Abhinaya Darpana:

Bhagawan Brahma taught Bharata the Natya Veda. Bharata along with the Gandharvas and Apsaras presented this art of Nritta, Nrutya and Natya before Bhagawan Shiva. There upon Shiva instructed his Ganas to teach Bharata his art of majestic performance and also requested parvathi to give instruction in lasya. Learning the tandava from Thandu the sages spread it to the mortals. Parvathi taught Usha the daughter of Bana, the lasya aspect of dance. Usha in turn, taught it to the gopis of dwaraka who taught it to the women folk of Saurastra. They spread it to the women of other countries. In this manner the art spread far and wide.

Brahma collected Pattyam, Gitam, abhinayam and rasam from Rig, Sama, Yajur and Atharva Vedas respectively to compile the Natya veda which enables one to achieve dharma, artha, kama and moksha, fame, intellect, self confidence and pleasure to dispel misery, sorrow and despondency.

IMPORTANT TEXTS ON DANCE

S. No	BOOKS ON DANCE	AUTHOR	TIME
1	Natya sastra	Bharata muni	BC 232 – SD 400
2	Abhinaya darpana	Nandikeshwara	BC 232 – SD 400
3	Abhinaya bharathi	Abhinava gupta	11 century
4	Dasharoopaka	Dhananjaya	10th century
5	Sangita Ratnakara	Sharanga deva	13th century
6	Bhava prakasha	Saradatanaya	11th century
7	Father of sanskrit drama – Kavya buddhacharita	Ashvagosha	2nd century
8	Bhavaprakasha	Saradatanaya	11th century
9	Mahabhasya	Patanjali	4th century
10	Sangeeta Makarandha	Narada	16th century
11	Malavikagnimitram, abhijnana shakuntalam, meghadutam etc	Kalidasa	4th century
12	Harshacharita	Banabhatta	7th century
13	Malathi madhavam	Bhavabhuti	8th century

S. No	BOOKS ON DANCE	AUTHOR	TIME
14	Shudraka, mritchakatika	Charudatta	6th century
15	Gita govinda	Jayadeva	12th century
16	Brihhadeshi	Matanga Muni	5th century
17	Kavya Mimamsa	Raja sekhara	9th century
18	Kavya Prakasa	Mammata Bhatta	11th century
19	Sringara Prakasha	Bhoja	10th century

S.NO	KANNADA BOOKS	AUTHOR	TIME
1	Lasya Ranjani	Simhabhupala	16th century
2	Adhunika Bharathadalli nruthya kale	U S krishna rao	
3	Nruthye kale	U S krishna rao	
4	Bharatanatya digdarshana	V S Koushik	

SHORT NOTES ON FEW TEXTS

<u>Natya Sastra</u>: The text, which contains 6000 slokas, is written by sage Bharata and is written during the period between 200 BCE and 200 CE (western dating system). Bharata is an acronym for the three syllables: bha for bhāva (mood), rā for rāga (melodic framework), and ta for tala (rhythm).

The Natyasastra of Bharata consists of thirty-six chapters in all. The first three chapters respectively deal with the origin of drama, the erection of theatre and the worship of the stage. Chapter 4 deals with the varieties of dance. Chapter 5 is devoted to the conduct of *purvaranga* or preliminary rites.' Chapters 6 and 7 relate to *rasas* (sentiments‖) and *bhavas* (emotions‖).

Chapters 8 to 14 (inclusive of 14)) are set apart for a discussion on *angikabhinaya*. The eight chapters from 15 to 22 deal with *vacikabhinaya* and related topics. In chapter 23 *aharyabhinaya* is treated. The next six chapters—from 28 to 33 (inclusive of 33) contain details about instruments and music. The last three chapters of the treatise, 34 to 36 (inclusive of 36) provide details regarding the different characters, varieties of costumes and popularization of the art of histrionics. This, in short, is the summary of the contents of the *Natyasastra*.

Natya Sastra is a science of drama, dance and music. This is the basis for all classical dance forms.

Abhinaya Darpana: Nandikeshvara (2nd CE – Western dating system, is the author of the Abhinaya Darpana (The Mirror of Gesture). Abhinaya Darpana is primarily followed by Bharatanatyam dance and it deals with chapters like Hand gestures, movements of various limbs, its usages, nava rasa (unlike Natya Sastra, which deals with 8 rasa), abhinayam, devatha hastas etc.

Dasarupaka: Dasharupaka is a treatise on Sanskrit dramaturgy, written by Dhananjaya in the 10th century AD – Western dating system. The author develops the subject from Bharata's Natyashastra. The Dasharupakam comprises four chapters, termed as Aloka.

Dasharupakam's main contribution to Sanskrit dramaturgy is a detailed analysis of the different types of heroines (Nayikabheda), and a critical study of Shringara Rasa. The writer has written ten types of Sanskrit dramas based upon the elements of Vastu (plot), Nata (heroes/heroines), and Rasa (the emotive aspect of plays). The dasarupaka explains 10 types of drama which are: Nataka, Prakarna, Samavakara,

Ehamruga, Dheema, Vyayoga, Prahasana, Bhana, Anka and Veethi. The most famous commentary on the work, known as Avaloka, was written by Dhanika, the younger brother of Dhananjaya.

CHAPTER 08

REPERTOIRE OF BHARATANATYAM

ALLARIPPU: The term allarippu has its origin from the telugu word 'allarimpu'. It is also known as Mohara or Addi. Allarippu belongs to nritta variety with emphasis on footwork and body movements. The item is divided into 3 phases each performed in 3 degrees of speed – vilambita (slow), madhyama(faster) and druta(fastest). The theme of the item is paying homage to the deity, to the learned and to the common people. The item is very shoty lasting for 3-5 minutes only. Here the dancer begins with Sama paada with her hands held above the head in anjali hasta. It is done is 5 different jathis. Angika abhinaya is given prominence in this item. It is the first item in a bharatanatyam repertoire. The purpose of performing this item first enables the body, limbs to get prepared for performing more difficult items subsequently.

JATHISWARAM: Jathiswaram which is usually presented as the second item in a bharatanatyam repertoire is difficult than allarippu. It belongs to Nritta category. In jathiswaram the rhythmic jathi patterns are interspersed with appropriate swaras. Hence the item is given the name Jathiswaram. Here we use a number of body postures with beautiful rhythmic song accompaniment. It is has no moods or sentiments. It produces an aesthetic pleasure of watching the dancer. Full sequences of adavus in different jathis like tisra, chatustra, khanda, misra and sankeerna are presented in jathiswaram. The song begins with a jathi, then continues with pallavi, anupallavi and charanam. The pallavi is sung many times for which different jathis patterns are choreographed.

DEVARNAMA: Devarnama literally means Name of God. Devaranama falls in Natya category. They are compositions of various devotees during the Bhakthi Movement in south india during the 13th to 14th century, especially in Karnataka. The objective was to promote dvaitha philosophy of Madhvacharya through literature. The saints who composed the devaranama were also called Haridasa. These compositions are in praise of the Hindu god Vishnu are called dasara padagalu (compositions of the dasas). These compositions can be more specifically categorized as keertanas,suladis,ugabhogas, and simply padas. They were easy to sing to the accompaniment of a musical instrument and dealt with bhakti (devotion) and the virtues of a pious life. Prominent Hindu philosophers, poets and scholars such as Sripadaraya, Vyasathirtha, Vadirajatirtha, PurandaraDasa and Kanaka dasa, Vadirajatirtha played an important role during this time. The compositions can be broadly classified under one of the following three types:

- *Kavya* or poetic compositions
- *Tatva* or philosophic compositions
- General compositions.

Each Haridasa had a unique *ankita nama,* or pen-name, with which they 'signed' all their compositions. The ankita nama of some of the most well known Haridasas is listed below:

Sripadaraya – Ranga Vittala, Vyasatirtha – Sri Krishna, Vadirajatirtha – Hayavadana, Raghavendratirtha – Dheera venugopala, Purandara dasa – Purandara Vittala, Kanaka dasa – Kaginele adikeshava.

Compositions are in many ragas and generally in Raagamalika and different Thalas. Eg: jaganmohanane Krishna, elli iruvano ranga, baro krishnayya, Bhagyadha lakhmi baramma, indhu yenege govindha.

CHAPTER 09

CHATHURVIDA ABHINAYA

"angiko vachikah tathva aharaya sattviko – aparah |
Chaturdhabhinaya tatra cha angiko – angaih nidarsitah | |
Vachavirachitah kavya nataka adhishu vachikah |
Aharyoharakeyura veshadibhiralamkrtah | |
Sattvikah sattvikaih bhavaih bhava jnena vibhavitah | |"

Abhinaya or Expressions is one of the most important factors in Indian dance. It literally means the representation or exposition of a certain theme. It is derived from Sanskrit **Abhi – to or towards, Ni – roots** or leading to. Bharata explains abhinaya as exhibiting the meaning of that which is depicted.

There are 4 aspects of abhinaya, which is also described in the sloka *"Angikam* bhuvanam yasya *Vachikam* sarva varmayam *Aharyam* Chandra tharadhi tham namaha *Sathvikam* shivam"

They are: Angika, Vachika, Aharya and Sathivika.

<u>**Angika Abhinaya:**</u> It is the language of expression through the medium of the body (sharira), the face (mukha) and movement (chesta). The angas are the major limbs, Pratangas and Upangas are the minor limbs. The main limbs when in movement will automatically utilise the minor limbs.

Anga – Anga consists of head, hands, chest, wrists and feet. There are 6 angas. Some authors also include neck as an anga.

Pratanga – This consists of shoulders, arms, back, thigh, belly. Others add 3 more such as waist, elbows and knees.

Upanga – This consists of eyes, eyesbrows, eyeball, cheek, nose, jaws, lips, teeth, tongue, chin are the upangas of the face alone. Heels, ankles, toes and fingers are few other upangas.

<u>Vachika Abhinaya:</u> The sacred treaties (Sastra) are formed from words. This verifies there is nothing beyond words. In classical dance, the singer gives expression to the words of song while the dancer interprets the meaning. This understanding between the musician and the dancer is of extreme importance. Apart from melodious voice of the singer, clarity is necessary in music and movements of dance, so that the audience can enjoy and understand each and every word that the dancer interprets. In some dance forms the dancer recites the verses on the stage aloud. Vachika is a vital factor as this makes understanding of the expressions easier. Vachika Abhinaya is extensively used in Drama and dialogue oriented art forms.

<u>Aharya Abhinaya:</u> This abhinaya is done through make-up and costume. In dance and drama, as soon as the character appears on the stage the physical form and figure is first noticed, then the words and then the acting is recognised. Hence Aharya abhinaya is significant for an immediate impression and a first expression.

The activity behind the curtain is broadly divided into 4 main aspects:

a) Pushta or set construction

b) Anga rachana or making up the face and body with paint etc.

c) Alankara or decoration

d) Sanjeeva or live presentation of animal or birds etc.

<u>Saathvika Abhinaya:</u> An actor might not have experienced what he/she is enacting on stage yet the actor has to portray or convey in a way that the audience understand it. That emotion which is felt, involuntarily or automatically exhibits itself outwardly, like tears or fainting. The word sattvika is endowed with the quality of sattva or purity. Sathvika abhinaya is depicting or acting a state of mind which has been caused by natural emotion. In kathakali and Kuttiyattam this abhinaya has been developed to the fullest. They hold a middle place between the sthayi bhavas and vyabhichari bhavas. Saathvika abhinaya is of 8 types:

1. Stamba – Still
2. Svedha – Sweating
3. Romancha – Thrill
4. Svarabedha – Trembling
5. Vepathu – Shivering
6. Vyvarya – Change in colour
7. Pralaya – Unconsciousness
8. Ashru – Tears

Rasa and Bhava:

"Vibhava anubhava vyabhichari bhava samyogaat rasa nishpathih"

It is the most important concept in Indian fine arts.

Vibhava → Anubhava → Vyabhichari bhava → Sthayi bhava → Rasa

Reason → Reaction → Passing state of mind/actions → Permanent state of mind → Rasa/Essence.

<u>Eg:1. Fear:</u> *Seeing Snake → Opening eyes → worry/death → bhayya → Bhayanaka.*

<u>2. Love:</u> *Seeing God → gentle smile → emotional/joy → Rati → Sringara.*

<u>Bhava:</u> The state of mind (chittavikara). The inner feeling which is felt is called bhava. According to Dhananjaya (author of dasarupaka) bhava means expressing the accumulated feelings in a unit manner. According to Natya sastra bhava means that which embodies words, anga and sattva. There are three types:

1.   Sthayi bhava – 8
2.   Sanchari bhava – 33
3.   Satthivika bhava – 8 = **Total = 49**

<u>Vibhava:</u> It is the reason or motive for bhava. Hence the origin bhava begins from vibhava. There are two kinds:

1.   Udhippana – Supportive reason
2.   Alambana – Main reason

<u>Anubhava:</u> It is the result or reaction of the bhava that has occurred. That which is felt afterwards is called anubhava. If the vibhava is the source of bhava, anubhva makes the bhava stand out prominently.

<u>Sthayi Bhava:</u> Stable or permanent state of mind. There are 8 kinds. The sthayi bhava remains constant from the beginning until the end.

<u>Vyabhichari bhava:</u> It means they come and go in aesthetic delight. That which appears and disappears according to the need of the act. They are 33 in number.

<u>Sathivika Bhava:</u> It is the potential state of mind. Sattva is something which arrives only when mind is calm and clear. They are 8 kinds as discussed above.

CHAPTER 10

NAVARASA

Rasa is the taste or essence of a work, an object or a piece of art. Rasabhinaya means the expression of ideas through sentiments or emotions. Rasa, that which is tasty, 'Svadheve rasa'. Intensive joy that is generated in a learned spectator due to his immersion or involvement in bhava is 'Svadha'. It is this Svadha which becomes Rasa. In Natyasastra, Bharatha has explained the concept of Rasa. The artist should be able to evoke, in the audience, the prominent rasas underlying in the piece. Rasa is that emotional feeling felt by one when he enjoys, hears or sees a performance or a piece of artistic beauty. This can also be felt whenever one reads a poetry, visualises a thing of beauty a scenery or hears a musical melody or a visual performance. It should be felt by oneself and not to be injected by anybody else.

According to Abhinaya Darpana, there are 9 rasas and according to Natyasastra there are only 8 rasas, Since Bharata did not approve 'shantha' as a rasa.

RASA	STHAYI BHAVA	DEITY	COLOUR
Sringara	Rati	Vishnu	Syama/Green
Hasya	Hasa/Hrushta	Manmatha	Sita/White
Karuna	Shoka	Yama	Kapota/Dove colour
Roudra	Krodha	Rudra	Rakta/Red

RASA	STHAYI BHAVA	DEITY	COLOUR
Veera	Utsaha	Indra	Gaura/Orange
Bhayanaka	Bhayya	Maha Kali	Krishna/Black
Bhibatsa	Jugupsa	Shiva	Nila/Blue
Adbhuta	Vismaya	Brahma	Pita/Yellow
Shanta	Shama	Bhuddha	NIL

"Sringara hasya karuna roudra veera bhayanaka |
Bhibhathsa adbhuta samjnau chetyashtau natya rasa smrutha | | "

The process of evoking rasa – – Bhavas are generated by vibhava and indicated by Anubhava and brought out by Vyabhachari bhava from which Rasa emanate.

Our ancients have prescribed particular colour, presiding deity and bhava for each rasa symbolically to infuse life into these rasas. It is believed that it is the Sthayi Bhava that results in various rasas.

<u>Extra Information:</u>

<u>Sringara: (Love)</u>

<u>Origin:</u> It is born from the pleasure of love. Its sthayi bhava is Rati. The love for whatever we see in this world.i.e. pure and radiant is known as Sringara. The vibhava is Alambhana – between 2.

Eg: Radha and Krishna

Anubhava: Anubhava is pleasure and happiness in the person.

Vyabhichari bhava: desire, joy, anxiety etc.

This rasa is divided into two:

- *Sambhogo – Love in union*
- *Vipralamba – Love in separation*

Hasya: (Humorous)

Origin: It is born from the emotion of humour. Its sthayi bhava is hasa. The vibhavas are strange way of dress, ornaments, quarrels, greediness, irrelevant talk etc.

Anubhava: Moving of lips, nose and cheeks, opening eyes wide, sweating, colour of face.

Vyabhichari Bhava: Joking, alasya, snoring and so on.

There are two types:

- *Athmastha – self created*
- *Parastha – seeing other objects*

This is further classified into six:

- *Smitha – smiling*
- *Hasitha – laughing*
- *Vihasitha – laughing with melodious sound*
- *Upahasitha – laughin by moving head and shoulder*
- *Apahasitha – laughing where one should not laugh*
- *Athihasitha – laughing by shedding tears, shaking entire body and loud sound.*

Karuna: (Pity)

Origin: It is born from the state of grief and sthayi bhava is soka.

Vibhava: Curse, affliction, loss of worldly goods, murder, sudden accidents and sadness.

Anubhava: Tears, crying drooping face and limbs, breathing deeply.

Vyabhichari bhava: Indifference, exhaustion, impatience, agitation, fear, terror. Nirvedha, glani, chints, asukhya, aavedha, moha, bhaya.

<u>Roudra: (Angry)</u>

<u>Origin:</u> It is born from the state of anger. Its sthayi bhava is krodha.

<u>Vibhava:</u> rakshasas, dhanavas, fighting, anger, false speech, offensive words, revenge and jealousy.

<u>Anubhava:</u> reddish eyes, nitting eyebrows, rubbing hands.

<u>Vybhichari Bhava:</u> Energy, ugly looks, indignation etc. Romancha, Amarsha, Ugratha, Garva, avega, chapalatha.

This rasa can be expressed in three kinds:

- By words(vak)
- By makeup (nepathya)
- By limps(anga)

<u>Veera: (Heroism)</u>

<u>Origin:</u> it is born from the state of energy, sthayi bhava is Utsaha.

<u>Vibhava:</u> composure, determination, prudent, conduct, power, courage, glory etc.

<u>Anubhava:</u> courage, anger, knowledge, awakening in knowledge, agitation, dignity etc.

<u>Vyabhichari bhava:</u> raising the eyebrow, standing up erect, calmness when required, intelligent talk, gait.

There are of three kinds:

- Veera (Courage)
- Dhanaveera (by charity)
- Udha veera (Fighting in war)

Bhayanaka: (Fearful)

Origin: It is born from the state of fear, sthayi bhava is bhayya.

Vibhava: Altered voice, seeing ghosts, fear from empty house, heights, forect, seeing death.

Anubhava: Shaking of hands, feet and eyes, pale face and change of voice, shivering etc.

Vyabhichari Bhava: depression, inconsistency, terror etc.

Bhibhatsa: (Disgust)

Origin: It is born from the state of disgust and its sthayi bhava is jugupsa.

Vibhava: these are bearing and seeing disagreeable and undesirable things.

Anubhava: Disgust in all limbs, face and eyes. Vomitting and spitting and shuddering.

Vyabhichari Bhava: Unpleasant sight, smell, taste, touch and sound resulting in disgution.

Adhbhuta: (Wonder)

Origin: It is born from the state of Wonder or astonishment, sthayi bhava is Vismaya.

Vibhava: sight of heavenly bodies, entering a garden, temple, magic or anything auspicious.

Anubhava: Opening eyes wide, starring, opening mouth, joyful tears.

Vyabhichari bhava: Wonderful speech, seeing beautiful image, deeds and forms.

This is of two types:

- *Divya (celestial)*
- *Ananda (Joyful)*

<u>*Shanta: (Peace)*</u>

<u>*Origin:*</u> *It is born from the state of tranquillity, sthayi bhava is sama.*

<u>*Vibhava:*</u> *control, restraint, recognition of truth, meditation, devotion.*

<u>*Vyabhichari Bhava:*</u> *Indifference, recollection, salvation, fulfilemt.*

Shanta rasa has been created to exclude all the worldly senses for it is the rasa for all universal beings and is a state of peace)

CHAPTER 11

HASTA MUDRAS

Asamyutha Hasta:

(Single Hand Gestures/Mudras)

Pathaka Tripathako-Ardhapathaka Kartari Mukhah |
Mayurakyo Ardhachandraschya Arala Shukathundakah ||
Mushtishcha Shikharakhyascha Kapitha Katakamukhah |
Soochi Chandrakala Padmakosha Sarpasirastatha ||
Mrigashirsha Simhamukhaha Kangula Alapadmakah |
Chathuro Bramaraschaiva Hamsasyo Hamsapakshakah ||
Sandamsho Mukulas chaiva Thamrachuda Trishulakah ||
ityasamyuta hastanam ashtavimsati ririta |

Samyutha Hasta:

(Double Hand Gestures/Mudras)

Anjalischa Kapothascha Karkataha Swathikastatha |
Dolahasta Pushpaputa Utsanga Shivalingakah ||
Katakavardhanaschaiva Kartari Swastikastatha ||
Sakata Samkha Chakrou cha Samputah Pasa Kilakou ||
Matsya Kurmo Varaha Garuda Nagabhandakah |
Katwa Bherunda Avihitaha stadhaiva cha ||
Chaturvinsati samkhyakah samyutha kathitah kara |

Viniyoga of Asamyutha Hasta:

(Usages of Single hand gestures)

Pathaka:

Natyarambhe Varivahe Vane Vastunishedhane | |
Kuchasthale Nishyayam Nadyam Amaramandale |
Turagge Khandane Vayou Sayane Gamanodhyame | |
Prathape cha Prasade cha Chandrikayam Ghanatape |
Kavat patane Sapta vibhaktyarthe Tarangake | |
Vithi pravesha bhavepi Samatwe Angaragake |
Atmarthe Sapathe chapi Thushnim bhavanidarsane | |
Talapatre cha Kheta cha Dravyadhi Darshane tatha |
Ashirwada Kriyayam cha Nrupasreshthasya bhavane | |
Tatra Tatreto Vachane Sindhou cha Sukritikrame |
Sambhodhethu Purogepi Khadga rupasya Dharane | |
Maase Samvatsare Varshadine Sammarjane tathe |
Evam artheshu yujyante pataka hasta bhavana | |

Meanings: Natya-arambe = beginning of dance, varivahe = cloud, vane = forest, vastu nishedhane = forbidding things, kuchasthale = breast, nisyaayam = night, nadyam = river, amaramandale = heaven, turage = horse, khandane = cutting, vayou = wind, sayane = reclining, gamana-udyame = walking, pratape = prowess, prasade = graciousness, chandrikayam = moon light, ghana-atape= scroching sunlight, kavata-patane = opening the door, sapthavibhakti-arthe = denoting the seven cases of grammer, tarangke = wave, vithipravesha bhave = entering the street, samatwe = equality, angaragake = applying sandalpaste etc, atmarthe = one's self, sapathe = taking an oath, tushnimbhava-nidarshane = sielnce, taalapatre = palm leaf, khete = shield, dravyadi-sparshane = touching the things, ashirwade kriyayam = benediction, nrpa-shreshthasya bhavane = a good king, tatra-tatra iti vachane = saying there and there, sindhou = sea, sukrtikrame = doing good things, sambhuddhe = addressing, puroge = going in front, khadgasya – rupa dhaarane = holding a sword, maase = month, samvastare = year, varsha dine = rainy day, sammarjane = cleaning (sprinkling water).

Tripataka:

Makute Vrikshabhave cha Vajre Taddhara Vasave |
Ketaki kusume Deepe Vahnijwala vrijumbhane | |
Kapole Patralekhayam Banarthe Parivartane |
Stripumsayoh Samayoge yujyate Tripatakah | |

Meanings: makute = crown, vrksha bhave = tree, vajre = vajra weapon, tat-dhara vasave = the holder of the vajra (lord Indra), ketaki kusume = screw-pine flower, deepe = light, vahni-jwala-vijrumbane = rising flames, kapole = cheeks, patra lekhayam = patterns drawn on the cheeks, bana-arthe = arrow, parivartane = turning round, stripumsayoh samayoge = union of women and man.

Ardha Pathaka:

Pallave Phalake Teere Apyubhayoh iti vachake |
Krakache Churikayam cha Dhwaje Gopura srngayoh | |
Yujyate ardhapatako ayam tattatkarma prayogatah |

Meanings: pallave = tender branch, phalake = writing or painting board, tire = bank of river, ubhayoh-iti-vachake = saying both, krakache = dragger/saw, churikayam = knife, dhwaje = flag, gopura-srngayoh = tower and horn.

Kartarimukha:

Stri pumsayostu visleshe Viparyasapade apiva |
Lunthane Nayane cha Marane Bhedabhavane| |

Vidyudarthe api ekasayya Virahe Patane Tatha |
Latayam yujyate yastu sa karah Kartarimukhah | |

Meanings: stri-pumsayoh visleshe = seperation of woman and man, viparyasapade – opposition or over turning, lunthane = stealing, nayana-ante = corner of an eye, marane = death, bheda-bhavane = disagreement, vidyut-arthe = lightening, ekasayyavirahe = reclining alone with pangs of separation, patane = falling, lata = creeper.

Mayura:

Mayurasye Latayam cha Sakune Vamane tatha |
Alakasyapa nayane Lalatatilakeshu cha | |
Netrasyodaka vikshepe Sastravade prasiddhake |
Evamartheshu yujyante mayura karabhavanah | |

Meanings: mayura-asye = peacock's beak, latayam = creeper, sakune = bird/omen, vamane = vomiting, alakasya – apanayane = stroking the hair, lalata-tilakeshu = forehead and tilaka on it, netrasya-udaka-vikshepe = wiping away tears, sastra-vade = discussion on sastras, prasiddhake = aspect of renown.

Ardhachandra:

Chandre Krshnashtami Bhaji Gallahastarthake-api cha |
Bhallayudhe devatanam abhishechana karmani | |
Bhukpatre Chodbhave Katyam Chintyam Atmavachake | |
Dhyane cha Prarthane chapi anganam sparshane tatha |
Prakrtanam namaskare apyardhachandro niyujyante | |

Meanings: krishna-ashtami bhaaji chandre = the moon on the eight day of dark fortnight, gala-hastarthake = seizing the neck, bhaa-ayudha = a spear, devatanam-abhishechana karmani = consecrating an image of God, bhuk-patre = plate used for eating, udbhave = origin or birth, katyam = waist, chintyam = musing one's ownself, atma vachake = one's self, dhyane = meditation, prathane = prayer, anganam sparshane = touching the limbs, prakrtanam namaskaare = greeting the common people.

Arala:

Vishamrutaadi Paneshu prachanda pavane api cha |
Yujyate arala hasto ayam bharatagama kovidaih ||

Meanings: Visha-amrta-adi paneshu = drinking poison or nectar, prachanda pavaneshu = violent wind.

Sukatunda:

Banaprayoge Kuntharthe Marma uktou Ugrabhavane |
Sukatunda karo jneyo bharatagama vedibhih ||

Meanings: Bana-prayoge = shooting an arrow, kunta-arthe = throwing a spear, marma-uktou = secret word, ugrabhavane = ferocity.

Mushti:

Sthire Kachagrahe Dardhye Vastuadhinam cha dharane |
Mallanam yuddhabhave cha mushti hasto ayamuchayate ||

Meanings: Sthire = steadiness, kacha grahe = grasping the hair, daardhye =firmness, vastu adhinam dharane = holding things, mallanam yuddhe bhave = wrestling.

Shikara:

Madhane Kaarmuke Stambe Nischaye Pitrakarmani |
Oshthe Pravishtarupe cha Radane Prasnabhavane ||
Linge Naathethivachane Smarane Abhinayaantare |
Katibandhakarshane cha parirambha vidhikrame ||
Sakti tomarayoh mokshe Ghantanade cha Peshane |
Shikaro yujyate so-ayam bharatagama vedibhih ||

Meanings: Madane = the God of love (manmatha), kaarmuke = bow, stambhe = pillar, nischaye = resolve, pitrakarmani = offerings to gratify the ancestors who are dead, osthe = lip, pravishta rupe = entering, radane = tooth, prasna bhave = questioning, linge = sivalinga, nasti-iti-vachane = saying no, smarane = recollection, abhinaya – antare = change in abhinaya, kati bandha akarshane = grabbing the girdle, parirambha vidhou = embracing, dhave = husband, sakti-tomarayoh mokshe = throwing sakti and tomara weapons, ghantaanaade = sound of bell, peshane = pounding.

Kapitha:

Lakshmyam chaiva Saraswatyam Veshatane Taladharane |
Godohane Anjane cha Lilakusuma dharane | |
Chelanchaladi grahane Patasya eva avagunthane |
Dhupa Dipa archane Chapi kapittah samprayujyate | |

Meanings: lakshmi = Lakshmi, saraswati = saraswati, veshtane = winding, taaladharane = holding cymbols, godahane = milking a cow, anjane = collyrium, liakusuma dharane = hoding flowers gracefully, celanchala – adi – grahane = grasping the end of a robe, patasya-eva-avagunthane = covering the head with a veil, dhupa-dipe-archane = offering incense and light.

Katakamukha:

Kusuma apachaye Mukta srak daamnaam dharane tatha |
Saramadhya akarshane cha Nagavalli Pradhanake | |
Kasturikadi vastunam peshane Ghandhavasane |
Vachane Drishti bhave api katakamukha ishyate | |

Meanings: Kusuma-apachaye = plucking flowers, mukta-srak-damnam dharane = wearing a pearl necklace or a garland of flowers, sara-madhya-akarshane = holding the arrow at the middle of the bow, nagavalli pradanake = offering folded betel leaves, kasturika-adivastunam peshane = preparing such things as musk etc, gandhavasane = applying scents etc, vachane = speech, dhrushti bhave = glancing.

Suchi:

Eka arthe api Parabrahma bhavanayam Shate api cha |
Ravou Nagaryam Lokarthe tatheti vachane api cha | |
yacchabde-api tacchabde vyajanarthe-api tarjane |
karsye salake vapushi ascharye venibhavane | |
kulala chakrabhramane rathange mandale tatha |
vivechana dinamte cha suchi hastah prakirtitah | |

Meanings: eka-arthe = one, parabrahma bhavanayam = parabrahma, sate = hundred, ravou = sun, nagaryan = city, loka-arthe = world, tatha-iti-vachane = saying thus, yat-sabde tat sabde = saying which and that, vyajana-arthe = fan, tarjane = threatening, karsye = thinness, salake = rod, vapushi = the body, ascharya = astonishment, venibhavane = braid of hair, chatre = umbrella, samarthe = capability, panou = hand, romalyam = the line of hair upon the abdomen just above the navel, berivadane = beating the drum, kulala chakra-bhramane = turning of the potter's wheel, rathange = wheel of chariot, mandale = circle, vivechane – thinking of pros and cons, dina-ante = evening.

Chandrakala:

Chandre mukha cha Pradeshe Tanmaatra kaaravastuni |
Shivasya mukute cha Ganga nadyam cha Lagude api cha | |
Esham Chandrakala chaiva viniyojya vidhiyate |

Meanings: chandre = moon, mukhe = face, pradese = the distance between the tips of the forefinger and thumb, tanmatra kaaravastuni = indicating a thing of the size of pradesa, shivasya mukute = jatajutam of Siva, ganga nadyam = river ganga, lagude = hand stick or cudgel.

Padmakosha:

Phale Bilwakapitthadhou Strinam cha Kuchakumbhayoh |
Avarte Kanduke Sthalyam Bhojane Pushpakorake | |
Sahakaara phale Pushpavarshe Majari kadhishu |
Japakusuma bhave cha Ghanta rupe Vidhanake | |
Valmike Kamale Apyande padmakoso vidhiyate |

Meanings: Phale = fruit, bilwa-kapitha – adou = bilwa-kapitha and other fruits, strinam kucha kumbhayoh = breasts, avartake = turning round or circular movement, kanduke = bal of flowers, sthalyam = plate, bhojane = food, pushpa-korake = bud, sahakaraphale = mango fruit, pushpavarsha = rain of fowers, manjarika – adishu = cluster of flowers, japakusuma bhave = the japa flower, ghantarupe – vidhanake = preparing big balls of food to feed the elephants, valmike = snake pit, kamale = lotus, ande = egg.

Sarpashirsha:

Chandane Bhujage Mandre Prokshane Poshanadhishu |
Devasya udaka dhaneshu Asphale gajakumbhayoh | |
Bhujasthane Mallanam tu yujyate sarpasirshakara |

Meanings: chandane = sandal paste, bhujage = snake, madre = slowness, prokshane = sprinkling, poshanaadishu = nourishing or cherishing, devasya udakadaneshu = offering water to gods, gaja-kumbhayoh = hitting the kumbasthala of an elephant, mallanam bhujasthane = arms of wrestlers.

Mrgashirsha:

Strinamarthe Kapole cha Chakra maryadayoh api |
Bhityam Vivade Nepathye ahwahane cha Tripundake ||
Mrugamukhe Rangavalyam Paada samvahane tatha |
Sarwa sammelane Karye Madhire Chatradharane ||
Sopane Padavinyasa Priyahwane tathaiva cha |
Samchare cha prayujyate bharatagama kovidaih ||

Meanings: strinam-arthe = matters pertaining to women, kapole = cheek, chakra maryadayoh = wheel and courtesy, bhityam = fear, vivade = quarrel or arguement, nepathye = costume and make up, ahwane = welcoming, tripundrake =three lines with vibhuti, mrgamukhe = face of a deer, rangavalyam = drawing patterns on the ground, padasamvahane = massage of the feet, sarwasammelane karye = grouping all, mandire = house, chatradharane = holding an umbrella, sopane = stairs, padvinyase = movement of feet, priya – ahwane = inviting the beloved, samchare = roaming.

Simhamukha:

Vidrume Mouktike chaiva Sugandha-alaka samsparshane |
Akarnane cha Prshati Moksharthe Hrdisamsthitah ||
Home Shashe Gaje Darbhachalane Padmadhamani |
Simhasane Vaidyapake Shodhane Simhavaktrakah ||

Meanings: Vidrume = coral, mouktike = pearl, sugandhe = frangrance, alaka – samsparse = stroking the curly hair, akarnane = hearing, prshati = a drop of water, hrdi samsthitah moksha-arthe = salvation, when the hand is placed on the heart, home = homam, shashe = hare, gaje = elephant, darbha chalane = waving kusagrass, padma damani = lotus garland, simha anane = lions face, vaidyapaka sodhane = testing the preparation of medicine.

Kangula:

Likuchasya phale Balukuche Kalhaarake tatha |
Chakore Kramuke Balakimkinyam GhutiKaadhike | |
Chatake yujyate cha ayam kangulakaranamakah |

Meanings: likuchasya phale = lime fruit, balukuche = breast of an young girl, kalhaarake = white water lily, chakore = patridge bird, kramuke = betel nut tree, bala kimkiniyam = little bells, ghutuka-adike = pill, chatake = chataka bird.

Alapadma:

Vikachabje Kapittha – adiphale cha Avartake Kuche |
Virahe Mukure Purnachandre Soundarya bhavane | |
Dhammile Chandra saalayam Grame Uddrtakopayoh |
Tataake Shakate Chakravake Kalakalaa rave | |
Slaghane Solapadmah cha kirtito bharatagame |

Meanings: vikachabje = full blown lotus, kapittha adi phale = wood apple etc, avartake = circular movement or whirl pool, kuche = breast, virahe = yearning for the beloved, mukure = mirror, purna chandre = full moon, soundarya bhavane = thinking about beauty, dhammille = hair knot, chandrasaalayam = moon pavilion, grame = village, uddhrta-kapoyoh = height and anger, tatake = lake, sakate = vehicle, chakravake = chakravaka bird, kala kala rave = "kalakalam" sound, slaghane = praise.

Chatura:

Kasturyam Kimchidapyarthe Swarna tamradi lohake |
Ardre Bhede Rasaswade Lochane Varna bhedane | |
Pramane Sarase Mandagamane Sakalikrte |
Asane Ghrta tailadou yujyate chaturah karah | |

Meanings: kasturyam = musk, kimchit-arthe = meaning a little, swarna – tamra – adi lohake = gold, copper and other metals, ardre = wetness, bhede = difference, rasa-aswade = experience of aesthetic pleasure, lochane = eyes, varna-bhedane = differentiating colours or castes, sarase = playful converse, pramane = oath, mandagamane = slow walking, sakalikrte = breaking to pieces, asane = high seat, ghrta – taila adou = oil, ghee etc.

Bramara:

Bhramare cha Suke Yoge Sarase Kokiladhishu |
Bhramarabhidha hasto ayam kirtito bharatagame | |

Meanings: bramare = bee, suke = parrot, yoge = practice of yoga, sarase = crane, kokila adishu = cuckoo bird etc.

Hamsasya:

Mangalye sutrabandhe cha Upadesha vinischaye |
Romanche Mouktikadou cha Dipavarti prasarane | |
Nikashe Mallikadou cha Chitre Tallekhane tatha |
Damse cha Jalabandhe cha Hamsasyo yujyate karah | |

Meanings: mangalye sutrabandhe = benediction and tying a thread during marriage, upadesa vinischaye = initiation and certainty, romanche = hottipilation, mouktika adou = pearl, dipavarti prasarane = extending the wick of a lamp, nikashe = touch stone, mallika adou = jasmine flowers etc, chitre = picture, tat lekhane = painting a picture, damse = gad fly, jalabandhe = dam, bindou = drop of water.

Hamsapaksha:

Shat-samkkhyayam Setubandhe Nakha rekha ankane tatha |
Pidhane Hamsa paksho ayam kathito bharatagame | |

Meanings: shat samkhyayam = number six, setubandhe = constructing a bridge, nakha-rekha – ankane = making marks with the nails, pidhane = concealment.

Samdamsha:

Udare Balidane cha Vrane Kite mahabhaye |
Archane Pancha samkhyayam samdamsa akhyo niyujyate | |

Meanings: udare = stomach, balidane = sacrificial offerings, vrane = tumour, kite = insect, mahabhaye = great fear or fear of death, archane = worship, pancha samkhyayam = number five.

Mukula:

Kumude Bhojane Panchabaane Mudra adi dharane |
Nabhou cha Kadali pushpe Yujyate mukulah karah | |

Meanings: kumude = water lily, bhojane = eating, panchabane = manmatha, mudra adi dharane = holding a seal etc, nabhou = navel, kadali pushpe = plaintain flower.

Tamrachuda:

Kukkutadou Bake Kake apyushtre Vatse cha Lekhane |
Tamrachuda karakhyo asou Kirtito bharatagame | |

Meanings: kukkuta-adou = cock etc, bake = crane, kaake = crow, ushtre = camel, vaste = child, lekhane = writing.

Trishula:

Bilwa patre Tritwa yukte Trishula kara iritah | |

Meanings: bilwa patre = bilwa leaf, tritwa yukte = three together or trinity.

Viniyoga of Samyutha Hasta:

(Usages of double hand gestures)

Anjali:

Devata guru vipranam namaskare shwanukramat |
Karyah Siro Mukha urasthah Viniyojyoanjalih budhaih ||

Meanings: devata guru vipranam namaskareshu = in saluting gods, elders or gurus and brahmins.

Kopata:

Pramane Gurusambhasha Vinayangikrtishwayam ||

Meanings: praname = bowing, guru sambhasha = conversation with guru and elders, vinaya angikrtishu = agreeing with humbleness.

Karkata:

Samuhagamane Tunda darshane Samkhapurane |
Anganam motane Sakhonnamane cha Niyujyate ||

Meanings: samuha gamane = arrival of group, tunda darshane = seeing or showing stoutness, samkha purane = blowing the conch, anganam motane = stretching or the cracking the limbs, sakha unnamane = bending the bough of a tree.

Swastika:

Makararthe Niyujyate ||
Bhayavade vivadecha kirtane swastiko bhavet ||

Meanings: makara arthe niyujyate = crocodile, bhaye vaade = timid speech, vivade = dispute, kirtane = praising.

Dola:

Natyarambhe Prayoktavya iti Natyavido viduh ||

Meanings: natyarambhe = starting dance

Pushpaputa:

Niranjana vidhou Variphaladi grahane tatha |
Samdhyayam arghyadane cha Mantra pushpe Niyujyate ||

Meanings: niranjana vidhou = offering aarati, vari phala adi grahane = receiving or collecting water, fruits etc, samdhyayam arghya dhane = twilight offerings (to the sun), mantra pushpa = at the time of chanting mantra pushpa (flowers).

Utsanga:

Alingane cha Lajjaya mangadadi pradarshane |
Balanam shikshane cha ayam utsanga yujyate karah ||

Meanings: aalingane = embrace, lajjayam = modesty or bashfulness, angada adi pradarshane = showing armlets, balanam sikshane = educating or disciplining the children.

Shivalinga:

Viniyogastu tasyaiva Shivalinga Pradarsane ||
Meanings: its use is in depicting shivalinga only

Katakavardhana:

Pattabhisheke pujayam Vivahasini yujyate ||

Meanings: pattabhisheke = coronation, pujyam = ritual or worship, vivaha ashishi = blessing at the time of marriage.

Kartari Swastika:

Sakhasu cha Adrishikare Vrksheshu cha niyujyate ||

Meanings: sakhasu = the boughs of trees, adri sikhare = the summit of a hill, vrksheshu = trees.

Sakata:

Rakshasa abhinaye Prayah Sakato viniyujyate | |

Meanings: rakshasa abhinaye = to denote rakshasas.

Samkha:

Samkhadishu Prayojayo ayam ityahuh bharatadayah| |

Meanings: in denoting samkha.

Chakra:

Chakra hastah sa vijneyah chakrarthe viniyuyate | |

Meanings: in denoting chakra.

Samputa:

Vastwacchede sampute cha samputah kara iritah | |

Meanings: in denoting concealment of things and a casket.

Pasa:

Anyonya kalahe pase srnkhalayam niyujyate | |

Meanings: anyonya kalahe = quarrel due to enmity, pase = noose, srnkhalayam = manacles.

Kilaka:

Snehe narmanulape cha kilako viniyujyate | |

Meanings: snehe = friendship, narmanulape = the conversation of lovers.

Matsya:

Etasya viniyogastu matsyarthe sammato bhavet | |

Meanings: fish

Kurma:

Kurma hastah sa vijneyah kurmarthe viniyujyate | |

Meanings: kurma

Varaha:

Etasya viniyogah syat varahartha pradarsane | |

Meanings: varaha

Garuda:

Garudo garudarthe cha yujyate bharatagame | |

Meanings: garuda

Nagabhandha:

Etasya viniyogastu nagabhandhe hi sammatah |
Bhujanga dampati bhave Nikumjanam cha darshane | |
Atharvanasya mantreshu yojyo bharata kovidaih |

Meanings: nagabhandhe = nagabandha, bhujanga dampatibhave = pairs of snakes, nikunjanam darshane = denoting bowers, atharwanasya mantreshu = atharwana mantra.

Khatwa:

Khatwa hasto bhavedeshah khatwadishu niyujyate |

Meanings: to denote bed and palanquin.

Bherunda:

Bherunda pakshi dampatyah bherundo yujyate karah | |

Meanings: to denote pair of birds or bherunda birds

Avahittha:

Srngara natane chaiva Lilakanduka dharane |

Kucharthe yujyaye so ayam avahittha karabhidhah | |

Meanings: Srngara natane = erotic dancers, lilakanduka dharane = holding a bal for play, kucha arthe = breasts.

CHAPTER 12

BHEDAS

SiroBheda
(Head Movements)

Sama Udwahita Adhomukhah Alolitam Dhutam ||
Kampitam cha Paravritta Utkshiptam Parivahitam |
Navadha Kathitam Sirsham Natyasastra visharadaih ||

Sama – straight facing head

Udwahita – Up

Adhomukha – down

Alolitam – rotating

Dhutam – left to right and right to left

Kampitam – up to down

Paravrttam – turning to one side

Ukshiptam – raising the head to one side (heroism)

Parivahitam – fast paced side to side (Shivering)

Drishti Bheda
(Eye Movements)

Sama Alokitam Sachi Pralokita Nimilite |
Ullokita Anuvratte cha tathachaiva Avalokitam ||
Ityashta Drishti bhedah syuh kirtitah purwasuribhih |

Sama – straight facing eye

Alokitam – rotaing

Saachi – side looking

Pralokite – side to side

Nimilite – looking at nose

Ullokita – up

Anuvrratta – up and down

Avalokitam – down

Bhru Bheda
(Eye-brow movements)

Sahaja patitokshipta Chatura Recita Tatha |
Kunchiteti Shadeva-atra bhru caturyavati kriyah | |

Sahaja – normal kept eyebrows

Patitha – bent down

Ukshiptam – raised up

Chatura – up and down

Rechita – one eyebrow up

Kunchethi – bent down and slight raised up (questioning with suspicion)

Griva Bheda
(Neck Movements)

Sundari cha Triaschina tathaiva Parivartitha |
Prakampita cha Bhavajnaih jneya griva chaturwidha | |

Sundari – side to side neck

Traischina – triangle shaped movement – diagonal.

Parivartha – moon or boat shaped movement

Prakampita – front to back like pigeon.

Pada Bheda
(Feet Movements)

Mandala Utplavana chaiva Bhramari Padacharika |
Chaturdha padabhedah syuh tesham lakshna muchyate | |

Mandala – the half sitting positions

Utplavana – jumping movements

Brahamari – rotating movements

Chari – Differents types of Gaits

CHAPTER 13

EXCERCISES AND YOGA FOR DANCERS

Exercise and yoga are essential for everyone, but dancers in particular should do them because they engage in a lot of mental and physical activity.

Knowing sixty-four different forms of other arts is a prerequisite for becoming a dancer! A dancer should practise yoga and other exercises every day to help with the quality and perfection of their dancing.

A dancer needs some essential attributes, and practicing yoga helps to develop them. They are as follows:

- Core strength and energy.
- Concentration
- Stamina and grip
- Mental potency and efficiency
- Creativity and swift results

Yoga poses assist the body in maintaining proper posture and helping the body stay in alignment.

VYAYAMA KRIYAS/EXCERCIES:

Taadakriya: Standing straight with karkata hasta hands held above the head.

Oordhawamukha kriya: Perform the taada kriya while balancing the body on toes with the neck stretched upwards.

Paarshwamukha kriya: Perfom the Taada Kriya while balancing the body on toes and bend the body at the waist on right and left sides.

Himmuka Kriya: Perform taada kriya and balance the body on toes and bend backwards.

Mummukha Kriya: Perform taada kriya while balancing the body on toes, exhale and bend forward to touch the toes.

Taadachalanam: Perform taada kriya while balancing the toes and walking in the front and in the back.

Uses: This kriya relieves the body of the painful araimandi position it is in during the dance. It relaxes the back, calf muscles, and thighs to allow for increased blood flow.

Jaanu Kriya: In standing position, the knee has to be slightly bent (like sitting in a chair poistion) and place the palms on the knees and rotate the knees.

Uses: This kriya is to strenthen the knees. The knee plays a major role in bharatanatyam dance. To maintain a strong knees, this kriya is very useful. It eases the knee muscles and keeps it flexible.

Aramandala Kriya: Keep the feet together while toes apart in a horizontal line and lowering the body height to its half. (araimandi position). Now keep the hands stretched above the head. There are four types:

1. Sitting in Araimandi and hands above the head parallel to each other.
2. Sitting → standing, alternatetively.

3. Sitting in araimandi and turn the upper part of the body from right side to left side.

4. Sitting in araimandi and turn the upper part of the body in a circular fashion like a mei adavu.

Uses: Aramandala kriyaa helps us avoid stiffness of the knee. Helps us to do Mei adavus and upper body movements. The position develops patience and will power. Since the araimandi is the primary position in Bharatanatyam, it contributes to the overall growth of dance.

Ardhakati Kriya:

Keep the feet together and slowly raise one hand above the head. Now bend the waist on the opposite side.

Uses: This helps in strengthening the waist and in turn creates angashuddhi. It facilitates in doing adavus with clarity especially those that have bending of waists like theermanam adavus etc.

Meru Vakra Kriya:

Stand with feet apart with good distant. Keep both the hands at shoulder level and bend the upper body front and back. Next turn right and left, keeping the feet and hands stable.

Uses: This kriya reduces fat in thigs, hips and arms. It also reduces the pain in back, neck or any muscle pull in the shoulders.

Hasta Paadothaana Kriya:

Stand erect and slowly lift right leg to waist level without bending the knee. Now touch the toes of the leg with the right hand while bending forward. Also, repeat the process on the left side.

Uses: This helps reduces knee pain and back pain. Also it avoids stiff limbs and fast execution of adavus.

Hasta Chaalana Kriya:

This kriya helps in easy movements of hands. This is of two types:

- **Manibandha kriya:** Form a fist and keep near the chest. Now rotate the fist inward and outward.

- **Varthula Kriya:** Keep Mukula hasta (joining all fingers at the tip of finger). Now place both the mukula hasta at shoulder and now rotate the elbow and move back and front while keeping the shoulder and back straight.

Uses: This helps in strengthening the wrists and shoulders. This inturn helps in holding neat and stiff mudras and natyarambam position, which is of vital importance in dance.

Greeva Kriya:

Sit on the floor in a comfortable position. Breath deeply (exhale and inhale) keeping your eyes half closed. During exhale create a humming sound from the throat. While humming, turn the neck in both the sides slowly.

Uses: This gives strength to the neck. Since neck is an important part of the body while dancing, this kriya helps to move the neck with ease.

Traatka:

The movement of the eyes is called Traatka. There are five types, they are:

- **Angushtha Traataka:** Stretch the right hand forward in front of the chest and out stretch only the thumb. (Mushti). Now stare at the right thumb.

- **Ungushtha Traatka:** Stretch the hand forward at chest with raised thumb in the front and move the hand from right to center and left to center. The eyes follow the right thumb.

- **Vaama Traataka**: Stretch the left hand forward with raised thumb in front. Now move the hand from left to center and center to right. The eyes follow the left thumb.

- **Vartula Traatka**: Stretch the right hand forward with raised thumb in the front and moved in circular movement. The eyes have to follow the thumb.

- **Ordhwa and Adho Traatka**: Stretch the right hand forward with raised thumb in the front and move it up to down and down to up. The eyes have to follow the thumb.

<u>Uses:</u> These kriyas give the eyes more glow, showcase bigger eyes and hence a clairty in expressions. Also, it relaxes the eyes. This also helps in concentration and memory.

ASANAS:

"Yoga is not just physical exercises, It's emotional integration, spiritual elevation, with the touch of a mystic element, which gives you a glimpse of something which is beyond all imagination."

~ Sri Sri Ravi Shankar

Yoga is a holistic science that integrates the mind, body, and spirit, as well as the cosmos. It makes everyone happy and at ease. It also significantly alters one's attitude, thoughts, and behaviour. Regular yoga practice improves our consciousness, intuition, sensitivity, and tranquilly.

As described in Patanjali's Yoga Sutra – "Sthira Sukham Asanam"– this means Yoga asana is a balance between effort and ease. We give effort to get into the posture and then we relax. Yoga asana brings that balance in every aspect of life.

Yoga is crucial for dancers since dance is similar to yoga. Therefore, it only benefits from regular yoga practice to maintain body and mind as one, which may enhance creative capacity, mental toughness, and a fit, healthy body.

There are many number of asanas, like Adho Mukha Śvānāsana (अधोमुखश्वानासन), Anantāsana (अनन्तासन), Ardha Candrāsana (अर्धचन्द्रासन), Dhanurāsana (धनुरासन), Eka Pada Kauṇḍiṇyāsana (एकपादकौण्डिण्यासन), Jānuśīrṣāsana (जानुशीर्षासन), Lolāsana (लोलासन), Mandalasana (मण्डलासन), Naṭarājāsana (नटराजासन), Tāḍāsana (ताडासन), Trikoṇāsana (त्रिकोणासन) and many others.

We shall discuss three below:

Vrikshaasana:

The name comes from the Sanskrit words *vriksa* or *vriksha* (वृक्ष, vṛkṣa) meaning "tree" and *asana* (आसन) meaning "posture".

First one comes to a straight position like the Tadasana, that is, legs standing together, both the hands parallel to the leg pointing downwards and head kept straight. Now with slow and deep breathes come to Vrikshaasana step by step.

How to:

The entire right sole of the foot is placed on the floor. The right foot is placed on the left inner thigh. The right knee should point sideways and not forward. The toes of the right foot should point downwards.

The centre of the left foot, the pelvic and the shoulder should be centrally aligned. The hands are held above the head and kept straight with hand clasped together in anjali mudra.

The asana is typically held for 20 to 60 seconds to stretch the spine, returning to tadasana while exhaling, then repeating standing on the opposite leg.

Benefits:

- Balance
- Poise
- Concentration
- Increases the range of motion in the hip
- Deepens the thorax
- Strengthens the ankles
- Tones the muscles of the legs, back and chest
- Posture

Pavana mukta asana:

This literally means wind-relieving pose or wind liberating pose.

The name comes from the Sanskrit words *pavan* meaning "wind", *mukta* meaning "relieve" and *asana* (आसन) meaning "posture" or "seat".

This asana is practiced in three stages:

1. In the first stage, the dancer lies on their back stretching the legs straight. Then bend the right knee and hold it with the hands, pressing it towards the abdomen. Breathing out, lift up the head and touch the knee with the chin. Breathing in, stretch the legs straight.

2. In the second stage, press the abdomen with the left leg.

3. In the third stage, press the abdomen with both legs, placing the chin between the knees. From this position,

swing the body back and forth 5 to 10 times, and then swing the body left to right and right to left 5 to 10 times.

The three stages above form one round. Three or four rounds would be ideal for good practice.

Benefits:

It helps in passing the gas, which might be blocked in the intestine. It creates space for fresh air in the body to create maximum utilization of the bodily resources. This improves the digestion system and helps have good motion.

Shavasana:

It literally means corpse pose. The name comes from the Sanskrit words *Shava* (शव, Śava) meaning "corpse" and *Asana* (आसन, Āsana) meaning "posture" or "seat".

To perform Shavasana, lie on the back with the legs spread as close as the ends of the yoga mat and arms relaxed to the side. Keep the eyes closed and breath deeply with the use of *deergha* (long) pranayama. The whole body is relaxed on the floor with an awareness of the chest and abdomen rising and falling with each breath. During Shavasana, all parts of the body are concentrated upon for muscular tension of any kind. Any muscular tension of the body is consciously released. All control of the breath, the mind, and the body is then released for the duration of the asana, typically 10–15 minutes.

The asana is released by slowly deepening the breath, flexing the fingers and toes, reaching the arms above the head, stretching the whole body, and exhaling while bringing the knees to the chest and rolling over to the side in a fetal position.

Benefits:

Shavasana is intended to rejuvenate the body, mind, and spirit. The deep breathes releases the stress. It makes one forget all other thoughts and surrenders any psychological effort. While in Shavasana, one slips into blissful neutrality and reflect on the practice.

CHAPTER 14

ADAVUS

Anga Shuddhi:

Anga shuddi means correct postures of the limbs which includes nritta hasta and Padabhedas. The elements of adavus are:-

1. Sthanaka
2. Chari
3. Nritta hastha
4. Hastha kshethra.

When these four elements are mastered, it is called as 'Angashuddi'. These are the essentials of 'Angashuddi'.

Dasavidha adavas.

1. Thattadavu
2. Nattadavu
3. Mettu adavu
4. Paraval Adavu/Rangakramana adavu
5. Egarutattu adavu – kudithu tattu
6. Egarumettu adavu – kudith mettu
7. Jaara adavu
8. Thattu mettu adavu
9. Mandi adavu
10. Theermanam adavu/mukthayi adavu

The lakshanas of an adavu.

Lakshanas of adavu: – (4 types)

1. Sthanaka

2. Chari

3. Nritta hastha

4. Hasthakshathra.

1) Sthanaka: – Starting posture of an adavu. Legs are kept 1 inch apart with the aramandi (half sitting). Required hastha mudras are holded.

2) Nritha Hastha: – Hastha mudras which are used while performing adavus. These does not convey any meaning.

3) Hastha Kshethra: – Starting & ending place of the hastha while performing adavu is called as hastha kshethra.

4) Chari: – Movements of hands and legs.

All these four elements together with Shirobeda (movements of head), Drishtibheda (movements of eyes), Grivabheda (movements of neck) & Brubheda (movement of eyebrows) are mastered and performed, with correct postures, then it is called to be Angashuddi.

Hasta Sthana:

Hastha Stana means sides of hastha or palms.

1. Uthana   :   Upside facing palm
2. Adomukha   :   Down
3. Unmukha   :   Hastha facing to our body
4. Paramukha :   Opposite to the body

Deha Sthana:

Position of the body

1. Sama: Both the feet are together and body is held straight. Here, araimandi also falls in this category, where in the legs are bent in half sitting position while the feet are places horizontally where the heels touch each other.

2. Aalida – One feet in araimandi and the other stretched like in naatu adavu (heel on the ground)

3. Pratyaaleda – one feet in araimandi and the other feet on the toes near to the first leg.

4. kunchitha jaanu – sitting down and balancing the body on the toes. (muzhumandi)

QUESTION AND ANSWERS

QUESTION PAPER – CLASS TEST

PORTIONS –

INDIAN CLASSICAL DANCES AND ORIGIN OF NATYA

I. ANSWER THE FOLLOWING 12*1=12

1. Write the meaning of the term Bharata.
2. Which element is taken from Rig Veda?
3. What are the classical dance forms of Kerala?
4. What is the name of the jewellery worn by Orissi dancers?
5. Write the names of dances styles of Manipuri?
6. Name the dance form which got its classical status in the year 2000.
7. Kuchipudi originated from which part of the country?
8. Bharatanatyam – the name first found its mention in which tamil texts?
9. From which word did kathak dance form gets its name?
10. What are musical instruments used in Bharatanatyam?
11. Through whom did bharata popularize Natya/nritya?
12. From whom bharata learns Lasya?

II. FILL IN THE BLANKS 12*1=12

1. ___________ brought the renaissance of Manipuri.
2. Nritta is ___________.

3. Tanjore brothers were appointed in the courts of __________.

4. Bhama kalapam is popular dance item of __________.

5. Gotipua is a dance form from __________.

6. Devadasis of Orissi were called __________.

7. There are __________ main types of gharanas in Kathak.

8. __________ is a famous story depicted in kathakali.

9. The dance of the enchantress is literal meaning of __________.

10. __________ established Kerala Kalamandalam.

11. __________ predominant in Mohiniattam.

12. Kinkini means __________.

III. ANSWER IN ONE SENTENCE. 10 *2=20

1. Name any four classical dance forms of india.

2. Write a guru in Bharatanatyam mention his place and style.

3. Write about Kathakars.

4. Write the names of three styles of orissi dance.

5. Write the first sloka from Natya Sastra.

6. Name the types of Vrittis.

7. Mention the names of the Gharanas of kathak.

8. Name the Jewellery used in Bharatanatyam.

9. Mention the name of the Tanjore quartet.

10. Mention a few names from the repertoire of Kathak.

IV. ANSWER THE FOLLOWING 8*3 = 24

1. Write the repertoire of Bharatanatyam.

2. Write a short note on Mohiniattam.

3. Write about Tarangam.

4. Why is Natya Veda called as Panchama veda?

5. Write about the Nepaathya used in Kathakali.

6. Name the Kings who patronised & promoted Bharathanatyam.

7. Explain the methods employed for learning Bharatanatyam.

8. What made Brahma create Apsaras?

V. ANSWER THE FOLLOWING 4*5=20

1. How did Brahma create Natya Veda?

2. Write a short note on Sattriya.

3. Name the classical dance forms of india and mention the names of the costumes used in each of the dance forms.

4. Write a short note on Manipuri.

5. Write about the Origin of Dance according to Abhinaya Darpana.

CLASS TEST – 2

PORTIONS –

LAKSHNAAS, CHATHURVIDA ABHINAYA AND NAVARASA

Marks 100
Hours – 2 ½ Hrs

I. ANSWER THE FOLLOWING 12*1 = 12

1. What is the meaning of Kinkini?

2. What is a Nati?

3. Name the chaturvida abhinaya.

4. What is the sthayi bhava of Sringara?

5. What is the meaning of Apatra?

6. What is the derivative of Abhinaya?

7. How do we derive Rasa?

8. What is hasya?

9. Who wrote abhinaya Darpana?

10. How should the dancing bells be?

11. Name any two rasa?

12. What is Uddipana vibhava?

II. FILL IN THE BLANKS 12*1=12

1. __________ is called external requisites of classical dance.

2. __________ is compared to a Sabha.

3. Vachika means __________.

4. Sthayi bhava of Roudra is __________.

5. Raso vai __________.

6. According to Bharata there are __________ rasa.

7. __________ is one of the sathvika bhavas.

8. Dancing without invocation is called __________.

9. The mixture of Sathyi bhava, vibhava and sanchari bhava creates __________.

10. Yatho __________ sthatho Rasah.

11. Abhinaya which is connected to noble feelings is called __________.

12. Being Stout is a __________.

III. A. Match the following 6*1=6

A B

a) Navarasa   i) Ornaments

b) Pity   ii) Natya

c) Abhinaya   iii) 9

d) Veera   iv) Shoka

e) Aharya   v) Reason

f) Vibhava   vi) Utsaha

B. Choose the correct answer: 6*1=6

1. Disgusting means

   a) karuna   b) shringara   c) bhibhatsa   d) hasya

2. To start dance program without salutation is

   a) natyakrama   b) neechanatya lakshana
   c) bahi prana   d) anthah prana

3. sveda, stambha, vaivarya are few examples of which abhinaya?

   a) angika   b) vachika   c) sathvika   d) aharya

4. Navarasa are mentioned in which book

   a) natya sastra   b) Sangita ratnakara
   c) abhijanan shakuntalam   d) abhinaya Darpana

5. Shringara rasa is attributed to which God ?

   a) Manmatha   b) Shiva   c) Vishnu   d) Brahma

6. Kinkini is usually made of _______ metal.

   a) gold   b) copper   c) brass   d) iron

IV. ANSWER IN ONE SENTENCE 10*2=20

1. Explain about Sanchari Bhavas.

2. Write about Vachika Abhinaya.

3. Write the sloka for constituents of Rasa.

4. What are the Patra Bahih Pranas?

5. Write about qualifications of a dancer.

6. What is Rasa?

7. Write about disqualifications of a dancer.

8. What is Adbhuta rasa?

V. ANSWER THE FOLLOWING 8*3=24

1. What is Neechanatya lakshana?

2. Write the chathurvuda abhinaya sloka.

3. Write Patra anthah pranas.

4. Write about Nata Lakshnas. (hero characteristics)

5. Explain about Kinkini

6. Explain Angika Abhinaya.

7. What is Bhava?

8. Why is Aharya Abhinaya important?

VI. ANSWER THE FOLLOWING 5*4=20

1. Explain what constitutes a Rasa?

2. What is Natyakrama?

3. What is Sabha?

4. Explain Sathvika abhinaya.

CLASS TEST – 3

PORTIONS –

LEGENDS OF BHARATANATYAM, LITERARY WORKS ON DANCE, DASAVIDHA ADAVUS AND EXERCISES

Marks – 100
Time – 2 ½ hrs

I. ANSWER THE FOLLOWING 12*1=12

1. Who is the author of Sangeeta Ratnakara?
2. What is Thaadakriya ?
3. What is Aasana?
4. Which is the encyclopedia of dance?
5. Who is the author of Lasya Ranjana?
6. Write any two works authored by Kalidasa?
7. Who are the Tanjore quartet?
8. Write about Mettu adavu?
9. How types of Aramandala kriyas are there?
10. What is the first adavu taught in a Bharatanatyam learning procedure?
11. What are the two important texts in Bharatanatyam?
12. Who popularized Pandanallur style of Bharatanatyam?

II. FILL IN THE BLANKS 12*1=12

1. _________________ is the guru of U S Krishnarao and Chandrabhagadevi.
2. N Gundappa is a disciple of _________.
3. _________ wrote Gita Govindam.

4. A close friend of raja Swathi Tirunal was __________.

5. Thei ya thei is the sollukattu of __________ adavu.

6. __________ kriye helps in strengthening the neck muscles.

7. __________ asana is good for complete relaxation of the body.

8. Nandhikeshwara has written __________ in Sanskrit.

9. Dasarupaka has __________ chapters.

10. The prominent disciple of Ramaiah Pillai is __________.

11. Puttadevamma was an artist in the court of __________.

12. In Kunchita janu, one should sit on __________.

III. MATCH THE FOLLOWING 6*1=6

A B

1. Adavu   i)   Eyes
2. Kalakshetra   ii) Basic steps
3. Narada   iii) 13
4. Nritta hastas   iv) Sangita Makaranda
5. Shutraadavu   v)   Rukmini arundale
6. Traataka   vi) Bramari

CHOOSE THE CORRECT ANSWER 6*1=6

1. Puttadevamma is a disciple of

    a) N Gundappa   b) Jatti Tayyamma

    c) Ramaiah Pillai   d) Chokkalingam Pillai

2. Natya means

    a) Abhinaya   b) pure dance

    c) combination of both   d) none of these

3. Pavanamukthasana helps in

   a) Relax thigh muscles   b) strenghthen body

   c) releases gas   d) flexibility of hands

4. The author of Dasarupaka is

   a) Simha bhoopala   b) bharatamuni

   c) Mohan Khokar   d) Dhananjaya

5. Who lived during the Sharobji maharaj times

   a) Narada   b) bhanubhatta

   c) Tanjore quartet   d) Mysore vasudevacharya

6. How many types of adavus are there?

   a) 3   b) 6   c) 10   d) 15

IV. ANSWER THE FOLLOWING 10*2=20

1. What is an adavu?

2. How many chapters and slokas does natya sastra contain?

3. To which province did N Gundappa and Chokkalingam Pillai belong?

4. How do we perform the egaru tattu adavu?

5. How does Vrikshasana help?

6. Name the prominent place where Venkatalakshamma worked?

7. What does Natyarambha mean?

8. What is the difference between kriya and asana?

9. What is Panchanadai?

10. What is a jathi?

V. ANSWER THE FOLLOWING 8*3=24

1. Name the Dasavidha adavus.

2. Give a list of authors of Natya during the ancient times.

3. How do we perform the jaara adavu? Explain.

4. Give a brief account on the life of Ramaiah Pillai.

5. What is the meaning of the term shollakattu?

6. How to do Ardhakati? Explain with usages.

7. Write a few books on natya written during modern times.

8. Which adavu comes as a finishing of a jathi? Explain it.

VI. ANSWER THE FOLLOWING 4*5=20

1. Write a short note on Natya sastra.

2. What is Anga Shuddhi? What are the elements of an Adavu?

3. How do biographies of dancers inspire you?

4. How does performing exercises and asanas benefit a Bharatanatyam dancer?

CLASS TEST – 4

PORTIONS –

ARCHITECTURE OF KARNATAKA, MUSIC IN DANCE, HASTA MUDRAS, BHEDAS

Marks – 100

Time – 2 ½ hrs

I. ANSWER THE FOLLOWING 12*1=12

1. What is navarang?

2. How many aksharas are there in misra chapu thalam?

3. What do you mean by mudra?

4. What is greeva bheda?

5. What is shashabda kriya?

6. Give two names of composers of devernama.

7. To which category of musical instrument does ghatam belong?

8. Name any 4 Asamyutha hastas?

9. What is lagu?

10. What is Aalida?

11. What are the angas of ata thalam?

12. Name any two things that took place during the Gupta period.

II. FILL IN THE BLANKS 12*1=12

1. Virupaksha temple is in ___________.

2. Veena is a __________ instrument.

3. In shikara hasta the __________ is stretched out.

4. There are __________ number of asamyutha hastas.

5. We find Madanikas in __________ temple.

6. There are __________ total number of thalas.

7. Shiro bhedas are movement of __________.

8. Gupta period is called __________.

9. Thaka tha kita is __________ nadai.

10. __________ is the father and __________ is the mother of Indian music.

11. In Kunchitha janu we balance our body on the __________ touching the ground.

12. The ascending order of swaras in music is called __________.

III. MATCH THE FOLLOWING 6*1=6

A B

1. Nritta hastas — i) 10
2. Samyutha hastas — ii) 9
3. Dhrishti bhedas — iii) 13
4. Shiro bhedas — iv) 24
5. Adavus — v) 4
6. Hastastanas — vi) 8

IV. CHOOSE THE CORRECT ANSWER 6*1=6

1. One can find shilabhanjike in which temple

    a) hoyasaleshwara b) hampi

    c) chennakeshava   d) Vijaya vittala temple

2. 'Ri' in swara stands for

    a) Rishabha   b) Rig   c) Rithi   d) Ritu

3. In which hasta viniyoga do we show mirror

    a) pathaka   b) tripataka

    c) Chandrakala   d) alapadma

4. What do the hoyasala temple buildings in Karnataka resemble in shape?

    a) pentagon   b) octagon   c) sun   d) star

5. Rechitha in bhru bheda is

    a) raising both   b) lowering both

    c) raising one   d) keeping normal

6. What is the name of hoyasala king Vishnuvardhana wife?

    a) Shakuntala devi b) Shanthala devi

    c) Sri devi   d) Shanthi devi

V. ANSWER THE FOLLOWING 10*2=20

1. In olden days what are the instruments used in Bharatanatyam?

2. Name the five varieties of thala.

3. Name three temple which are known for dance sculptures.

4. Name some Shilabhanjikas.

5. What are the uses of Anjali hasta?

6. What is the difference between prakampita and parivartita greeva bhedas?

7. Write a small note on Jathiswara?

8. What is meant by shiro bhedas? Name them.

9. What are the benefits of dance?

10. What is importance of music in dance?

VI. ANSWER THE FOLLOWING 8*3=24

1. What is raga?

2. Name the temples built by chalukyas and give their date.

3. What are the lakshnas of Allarippu?

4. Write any 5 usages of mushti hastas. And its lakshanas.

5. How many kinds of musical instruments are there? Name them.

6. Why are sculptures so important for art/How is dance and sculptures related?

7. What is the difference between samyutha hastas and nritta hastas?

8. Write lakshanas of any 3 samyutha hasts.

VI. ANSWER THE FOLLOWING 5*4=24

1. What is thala system followed in Carnatic music. Explain

2. What are the dhrishti and Bhru bhedas. Name them with usages.

3. What are the different kind of sculptures found in karanataka. Explain.

4. What is hasta sthana and dehasthana?

JUNIOR GRADE

SAMPLE I – QUESTION PAPER

Theory

I. Answer the following: 12 * 1 = 12

1. What is the meaning of the term 'Bharata'?

2. Which element is taken from Rig Veda ?

3. How many Shirobhedas are there according to Abhinaya Darpana ?

4. What is Abhinaya ?

5. What is Samapada ?

6. What is Samyuta Hasta ?

7. What is Adavu?

8. What is Nrutta ?

9. What is Aramandi ?

10. What is Asana ?

11. What is Arbhativritti ?

12. What is Tattadavu ?

II. Fill in the blanks: 12 *1 = 12

1. Cymbals (Natuvanga) are the examples of __________ Vadya.

2. Jatiswara belongs to __________ category.

3. Panchama Veda is __________

4. Pataka Hasta belongs to ___________ Hasta.

5. Kinkini means __________

6. Alaripu belongs to __________ category.

7. Author of Abhinaya Darpana is __________

8. __________ is predominant in Mohiniattam.

9. __________ Abhinaya is performed with make-up.

10. Gupta period belongs to __________ age.

11. __________ was the student of Jatti Tayamma.

12. Nandikeshwara has compared 'Sabha' with __________

III. A. Match the following: 6 * 1 = 6

a) Alaripu   i) Andhra Pradesh

b) Jatti Tayamma   ii) Rasa

c) Dasharupaka   iii) Mysore

d) Veera   iv) Nrutta

e) Kuchipudi   v) Dhananjaya

f) Devaranama   vi) Abhinaya

B. Choose the right answer: 6 * 1 = 6

1. Jatiswara is

    a) Natya   b) Nrutta   c) Rasa   d) Lasya.

2. Violin is __________ instrument.

    a) Tata   b) Sushira   c) Avanaddha   d) Ghana.

3. Looking straight means

    a) Sama   b) Sachi   c) Anuvrutta   d) Avalokita.

4. Kathakali is the dance form of

    a) Karnataka   b) Kerala

    c) Andhra Pradesh   d) Maharashtra.

5. Group of Adavus is

a) Nruttabandha   b) Pataka Hasta   c) Korve   d) Jati.

6. Pataka Hasta is

a) Samyuta   b) Greevabheda   c) Asamyuta   d) Vyayama.

IV. Answer the following in *two* sentences each: 10 *2 = 20

1. How many Jatis are there? Name them.

2. Mention the famous Nritya Shilpas in Karnataka.

3. What are the differences between Shirobhedas and Greevabhedas?

4. How many Vedas are there? Name them.

5. What is devaranama?

6. What are Samyuta and Asamyuta Hastas?

7. Write the Angas for Khanda Jati Atta tala & Tishra Jati Triputa tala.

8. Write one of the famous Gurus in Bharatanatyam & mention his place and style.

9. What is the difference between Nrutta and Nrutya ?

10. How many Vruttis are there in Natya ? Name them.

V. Answer any *eight* of the following: 8 * 3 = 24

1. Write the names of three books and their authors belonging to Bharatanatyam.

2. Explain the features of Udvahita and Dhuta Shirobhedas.

3. Explain brifely the features of Alaripu.

4. Write the names and period of Tanjore Brothers.

5. Write about 'Kinkini' Lakshana according to Abhinaya Darpana.

6. What are the advantages of learning Dance ?

7. Explain how Khatwa and Berunda hastas formed.

8. Write the origin of Natya Shastra.

9. Write briefly about Jatiswara.

10. Which are Dasavidha Adavus ?

VI. Write any *four* of the following: 4 * 5 = 20

1. Why did Brahma created Apsaras ?

2. Explain the method to create Hastapadotthana kriye.

3. What is meant by Alaripu ? Explain its Lakshanas.

4. Explain any five Samyuta hasta Lakshanas.

5. Write briefly about Natya Sastra.

SAMPLE QUESTION PAPERS

(English Version)

$12 \times 1 = 12$

Answer the following in a sentence each :

1. What is Nritta ?
2. What is Asana ?
3. What do you mean by Kinkini ?
4. What is a chāri ?
5. What do you mean by anchita pāda ?
6. What is meant by Adhomukha ?
7. What is the feature of Tripatākā ?
8. Name any two string instruments (Tat Vādya).
9. Which is considered as the encyclopedia of Dance ?
10. Name any two temples where you find the sculptures of dance.
11. What is "Anudruta" ?
12. What is Satwathi Vritti ?

Fill in the blanks with appropriate words :

$12 \times 1 = 12$

1. .... was a great dancer who was the queen of Vishnuvardhana.
2. In various temples of Karnataka we can find a circular stage in front of main statue of god called ....
3. .... created Panchamaveda.
4. The Asana that provides rest to the body is ....
5. Yatho Manastato ....
6. Anchita Pāda placed in front is ....
7. According to Bharata threre are .... Rasas.
8. The Bharatanatyam style of Mugur Jejamma is famous as .... style.
9. Dancing without the invocation is called ....
10. .... is predominant in Mohiniattam.
11. Lasya Ranjana was written by ....
12. Series of Adavus with Teermana is ....

Answer the following in *one* sentences each :   10 × 2 = 20

1.   Name any *four* classical dances of India.

2.   Name any *four* internal needs of Antapranas of a dancer.

3.   Write the *four* features of Adavus.

4.   What is meant by "Aramandi" and "Kunchita Janu" ?

5.   Name Tanjore brothers.

6.   Whose disciple was Chokkalingam Pillai ? Name his style of Dance.

7.   What is the difference between Kuditta Tattadavu and Kuditta Mettadavu ?

8.   What is Devaranama ? What are the writers of Devaranama called ?

9.   Name the dance items of lineage of Bharatanatyam or margam of Bharatanatyam.

10. Name Drishti Bhedas.

Answer any *eight* of the following :   8 × 3 = 24

1.   Explain Kinkini Lakshana.

2.   Write about Hasta Chalana Kriye.

3.   Name the Shirobhedas.

4.   Write the Hasta Lakshana of the following Hastas.

     Trishula, Ardha Pataka, Hamsasya.

5.   What is Raga ? Explain.

6.   Explain the classification of musical instruments with an example for each.

7.   How did Brahma create Natyaveda ?

8.   What is Trikāla ? Explain.

9.   Name the Dashavidha Adavus.

10. Write a short note on Abhinaya Darpan.

VI. Answer any *four* of the following :

1. Write the uses of learning dance.

2. What is Chaturvidha Abhinaya ? Explain.

3. Explain Sapta Talas with their Angas and symbols.

4. Explain about the five Jatis of Tala.

5. Explain any two Asanas with its usage.

SAMPLE QUESTION PAPER

Answer the following questions :   12 × 1 = 12

1.   What is Nrutya ?
2.   What is Thadachalane ?
3.   To which state does Manipuri dance form belong ?
4.   Name the direction of Parangmukha hasta.
5.   What is Arabhati Vruthi ?
6.   What do you mean by Nruta Hasta ?
7.   What is Avarohana ?
8.   Who is the author of 'Lasya Ranjana' ?
9.   How many types of Swaras are there ?
10. Write one use of Nagabandha Hasta.
11. What do you mean by Jati ?
12. What is Sushira Vadya ?

Fill in the blanks with appropriate words :   12 × 1 = 12

1.   Famous style of V. Ramaiah Pillai is ....
2.   Author of the Kannada book 'Nruthya' is ....
3.   The Anga of .... tala is 1 Laghu and 2 Drutas.
4.   Veena is a .... instrument.
5.   Abhinaya which is connected to noble feeling is ....
6.   Devaranama belongs to .... category of dance.
7.   Moving eyeballs from one side to another side is called ....
8.   Stretching the thumb of Musti hasta upwards is ....
9.   Natya Shastra has .... number of chapters.
10. The adavu that covers the full stage is called .... adavu.
11. Kinkini means ....
12. The limb movement is called ....

III. A.   Match the following :

A		B	
a)	Nataraja	i)	Nrutha
b)	Alaripu	ii)	Rasa
c)	Veera	iii)	Shastreeya Nrutya
d)	Odissi	iv)	Dhananjaya
e)	Abhinaya Darpana	v)	Natyadhidevathe
f)	Dasharupaka	vi)	Abhinaya
		vii)	Nandikeshwara.

B.   Choose the correct answer and complete the following sentences :

6 × 1 = 6

1)   "Sa" means ....

   a)   Rishabha   b)   Gandhara

   c)   Shadja   d)   Nishada.

2)   Devaranama is ....

   a)   Nrutha   b)   Nrithya

   c)   Natya   d)   Tandava.

3)   .... is a Tathavadya.

   a)   Mrudanga   b)   Ghatam

   c)   Flute   d)   Violin.

4)   Circular eye movement is ....

   a)   Dhuta   b)   Kampitha

   c)   Alokitha   d)   Awalokitha.

5)   Anjali hasta is ....

   a)   Samyuta   b)   Asamyuta

   c)   Nrutta   d)   Abhinaya.

6)   Kinkini means ....

   a)   Tala   b)   Laya

   c)   Bells   d)   Raga.

Answer the following in *two* sentences each :

1. Explain the difference between Nrutha and Nruthya.

2. Name the classical dance of North India. Where is it prevelant ?

3. What is meant by Samyuta and Asamyuta Hastas ?

4. Name a famous dance exponent with his style and region.

5. Mention the characteristics of any two Adavus.

6. How many Vruthis are there ? Name them.

7. Mention any two Talas along with their Angas.

8. Mention any two temples of Karnataka with dance sculptures.

9. What is Meruvakthrakriye ?

10. Indicate the difference between Shirobheda and Greevabheda.

Answer any *eight* of the following questions :   8 × 3 = 24

1. Mention three treatises pertaining to dance. Indicate their names and period.

2. Mention the Kinkini characteristics of Abhinaya Darpana.

3. Mention the characteristics of Alaripu.

4. What is meant by Vachikabhinaya ? Explain.

5. Explain the difference between Udhwahitha and Dhrutha Shirobheda.

PRACTICAL PAPER I

Max marks 100

1. Mention any 2 usages of ardhachandra, arala, shukathunda, mushti and shikara. (15)

2. Mention any 3 usages of any five Samyutha hasta of student's choice. (15)

3. Demonstrate the allarippu with thalam. (15)

4. Sing – sarali varise and Janti varise. (15)

5. Sing any one Alankara. (15)

6. Sing the devernama. Explain what is devernama. Mention its raga, thala and composer and bhava Artha. (15)

PRACTICAL PAPER II

Max marks 150

1. Perform any 2 yoga asana and mention its usages. (20 marks)

2. Perform the Jaar adavu and Kudith Mettu adavu. (20)

3. Show the greeva and shiro bhedas and explain its usages. (20)

4. Name the saptha thalas and tell angas of 2 thala.

5. Perform Allarippu – first half in tisra and second half in chatusra and describe allarippu. (20)

6. Perform jathiswaram and explain about the item (20)

7. Perform Devernama.

VIVA VOCE

Max marks 50

(Examiner will demonstrate in the class the below questions)

1. Examiner to demonstrate the below rasa and student have to identify and write the rasa in their answer sheet (4*2=8)

   a) sringara   b) roudra
   c) bhayanaka   d) karuna

2. Examiner to perform adavu. Student to identenfy (4*2=8)

   a) mettu   b) kartari
   c) rangakrama   d) mandi

3. demonstrate the Thalam (3*2=6)

   a) Dhruva tisra   b) roopaka khanda   c) triputa misra

4. demonstrate the hasta and and student to write any 2 of its viniyoga (4*2=8)

   a) mayura   b) mushti
   c) utsanga   d) nagabhandha

5. Demonstrate the below bhedas (4*2=8)

   a) pralokita – dhrishti   b) udwahita – shiro
   c) sundari – greeva   d) utkshipta – bhru

6. Demonstrate the below kriye. Student to identify and write its usgaes (3 *2=6)

   a) jaanu kriye   b) meru vakra   c) greeva kriye

7. Examiner to sing any Roopaka thala jathiswara. (2*3=6)

   a) student to write which nritya bhandha
   b) and which thala

SENIOR

TABLE OF CONTENTS

SYLLABUS OF SENIOR BHARATANATYAM EXAMINATION

THEORY
PAPER 1

Classical dance forms of India *(refer Junior)*

Definitions

The glory of Nataraja Murthy

Hasta Mudra (with Slokas of Viniyoga) *(refer junior)*

Paada bhedas

Chaturvidha abhinaya

Repertoire of Bharatanatyam

PAPER 2

Thaala Prakaranam

Raaga lakshanam

Aharya Abhinaya

Musical instruments *(refer Junior)*

Folk dances of Karnataka

Life history of legends

PRACTICAL
PAPER 1

Hasta viniyogas

Thala prakaranam

Singing of dance numbers

Taana varnam

PAPER 2

Adavus in Trikala and Pancha Jaathi

Kouthuvam

Allarippu – 4 (tisra, chaturasra, khanda, misra)

Jathiswaram – 4

Shabdam – 1

PAPER 3

Pada varnam – 1

Padam – 2

Jaavali – 2

Krithi – 1

Devernama – 2

Thillana – 2

Shloka – 2

Laghunritya – 1

CHAPTER 01

DEFINITIONS

NATTUVANGAM: Nattuvangam is a tamil word i.e. Natta and Angam. Natta means dancer and angam means body or main operating. It is made of metal alloys. The sounds produced by tapping the cymbols at various angles represent the different sounds of the dancer's feet when they mae contact with the ground. of the two cymbols the larger one that produces the bass sound is made of iron, while the treble sound comes from the brass cymbol. According to the mridangam and the song, the nattuvanar or the guru plays the cymbols in different jathis to support the dancer or the student by reciting the jathis (sollu-kattu), this is known as nattuvangam. Dancer completely depends on the support of the nattuvangam. It is the main component in a program. some of the great exponents of playing nattuvangam are G.Elagovan, Seetaram Sarma, Adyar K Lakshman.

NATYA: The word natya is derived from the word Nat, moving or acting. Natya means dramatic representation or drama with music and dance. The ancient theatre has evolved according to the rules of laid by bharata. In natya there will be different characters, each character will have set instructions, giving interesting insight into the art form.

NRITYA: Nritya is that manifestation of dancing which includes both Rasa (aesthetic flavour) and Bhava(emotion). In Nritya there need not be different charactors played by different roles. One individual can play all roles and express the meaning of the song with adeptness.

NRITTA: Nritta is a form of pure movement in dance which while reflecting the mood of the musical composition does not utilize on sentiments (rasa and bhava). This dance is the combination of different kinds of footwork, body, hand, head and eye movements.

ABHINAYA: It literally means the representation or exposition of a certain theme from. It is derived from the Sanskrit words, Abhi – To or towards – with root. Ni – to lead. Bharat explains abhinaya as exhibiting the meaning of that which is depicted. It has four aspects namely angika, vachika, aharya and sathivika. Angika is the language of expression through medium of body. Vachika is the expression through words. Aharya is the expression through decoration and sathvika is the expression through state of mind.

ADAVU: An adavu is the combination of movements of hands and footwork in a dance. The dancer begins learning the basic dance steps called adavus. Its elements are sthanakas (poses), chaaris (movements). In adavus, particular importance is attached to anga shuddha (correct postures of the limbs) which includes nritta hastas and pada bhedas, tala shuddha. These form the structured dance of thadava (strong movements) and lasya (graceful movements).

The adavus when combined is called Jathis (group of steps/ adavus) and theermana is a ending combination of Jathis. Aradhi is a ending sequence in a theermana).

Adavu forms the foundation on which the entire nritta rests. It must have evolved from karanas. In dance, especially the nritta portion, adavus are inter woven artistically and beautifully forming the pure dance movements. The combination of several adavus creates fascinating patterns of great visual and sculptural beauty.

JATHI: This is a combination of 2 or more adavus with complicated footwork and hand movements always ending with a theermana. This will generally be in three speeds.

MUKTHAYI: Mukthayi is presented before the starting (which is mostly not danced) and at the finishing of dance. Generally Mukthayi is very small. Eg: tha ding gina thom.

THEERMANA: This means the conclusion. It is a movement ending a group of movements and is usually repeated thrice. Generally this will be in 5 jathis. Mostly it is done in thillana, jathisawaram or any jathis. Eg: tha ding gina thom, thaka tha ding gina thom, thaka dhiku tha ding gina thom.

LASYA: The feminine form of dance is lasya which believed to have been introduced by Goddess Parvathi. Lasya aspect of dance strengthens the spiritual fervour of shiva thandava. It is composed to delicate karanas, possess graceful bodily movements. Lasya is the dance form performed by Apasaras. It is mainly of four types: Srikala, Lata, Pindi and Bhedyaka.

THANDAVA: Thandava is composed of various movements, posses strong bodily movements. It is believed to have been introduced by Thandu, lord of this dance is Shiva. This is of 3 classification: Udhathanrutha, Udhathanruthya, Udhathanatya. Thandava is a combination of Angahara (32), Karana (108), Rechaka (4) and Pindibandhas (4).

BHARATHA: Bharatha Muni is the author of Natya Sastra. Bharata is considered the father of Indian theatrical art forms.

The Natyashastra comprises 36 chapters and it is possibly the creation of more than one scholar. It dates from between the 3rd century BCE and the 1st century CE. Bharatanatyam sometimes is also derived from the words Bhava, Ragam and Thalam to form Bharatha.

MARGI AND DESI: The Natya Shastra divides dance into various categories. On one hand we have the classical dance forms such as Bharatnatyam, Kathakali, Kathak and so on and on the other hand we have dances like garba, bhanga, chau and so on. Although these are all dances, they fall into two distinct categories, that is: Margi (Classical) and Desi (Folk or regional)

MARGI: All the dances that are classical and have specific stylised movements based on the tenets given by Bharat Muni in the Natya Sastra fall in the Margi category. They have a specifically designed and well thought repertoire that is carried out as a tradition. Special training is required to master these dance forms. The thematic content of the songs is mostly religious and oriented towards God.

Eg: Bharatanatyam, Kathakali, Kathak, Odissi, Mohiniattam, Kuchipudi and Manipuri, Satriya.

DESI: Dances falling in the Desi category are more regional and folkish in nature. They are oriented more towards the people and are popular. They are done majorly to entertain and celebrate and have little or no religious connotation. These folk dances are done in groups during special festivals, occasions such as marriage, harvesting seasons or fairs. The steps are generalised and simple and generally require no exclusive rigorous training. Everybody can participate. Every region or tribe has their own folkdance. Egs: Bhangra, Garba, Gidda, Chau, Rajasthani dance, etc.

SOLLUKATTU: Sollukattu is a tamil word, literally meaning, sollu – word kattu – structure. A rhythmic syllable, or phrase of rhythmic syllables (sollukattu) linked to specific units of dance movement (adavu). For example – thattu adavu sollukattu is *"thei ya thei "*.

RANGAPRAVESHA: The debut performance of a Bharatanatyam dancer, marking his or her readiness for performing a full solo recital. A Kannada word meaning to step onto the stage, from of *ranga* (stage) and *pravesha* (entry).

ANGASHUDDHI: Anga lakshana, the way body parts move, that is a combination of shirobedas, greevabedas, dhrishtibedas, padabedas, utplavana, brahmari, chari, gatibedas, hastas – when all these angas coordinate along with pratyanga and upanga, the artist is said to have Angashuddhi. Anga means body parts and shudhi means perfect. A dancer should strive to achieve this state.

CHAPTER 02

NATARAJA MURTHY

Bhagawan Shiva, the greatest dancer, who is known as cosmic dancer.

"Angikam bhuvanam yasya vachikam sarva varnmayam aharyam chandra thaaradhi thamnamaha satvikam shivam"

This interesting sloka explains that he truly is a cosmic dancer. The world as his attire, all the words as his speech, celestials as his ornaments, and that shiva in sattva is Nataraja.

Ananda Coormaraswamy quotes in his book 'The dance of shiva', "Whatever the origins of Shiva's dance, it became in time the clearest image of the activity of God which any art or religion can boast of. Of the various dances of Shiva is shall only speak of three, one of them alone forming the main subject of interpretation. The first is an evening dance in the Himalayas, with a divine chorus, described in Shiva Pradosha Stotra. The second well known dance of Shiva is called Tandava, and belongs to His Tamasic aspect of Bhairava or Virabhadra. It is performed in cemeteries and burning grounds, where Shiva, usually in ten-armed form, dances wildly with Devi, accompanied by troops of capering imps. Thirdly we have Nadanta Dance of Nataraja before the assembly in the golden hall of Chidambaram or Thillai, the centre of the Universe first revealed to Gods and Rishis after the submission of the latter in the forest of Taragam, as related in the Koyil Puranam. "

The dance represents the five activities of the universe (Panchakriyas).ie. shrishti, sthithi, samhara, tirobhava, anugraha which is represented by five Gods, Brahma, Vishnu, Rudra, Maheswara and Sadashiva respectively.

The Nataraja Murthy, where we find Him holding the drum, the fire, the wavy hair, hands in abhaya hasta, "mughizhavan" the demon under the leg, one leg raised up, each has a meaning to universe and its dance. We find this from Unmai Vilakkam, verse 36:

"Creation arises from the drum, protection proceeds from the hand of hope, from the fire proceeds destruction, the foot held aloft gives release."

The sculpture is usually made in bronze, with Shiva dancing in an aureole of flames, lifting his left leg (or in rare cases, the right leg) and balancing over a demon or dwarf (Muyalaka) who symbolizes ignorance. It is a well-known sculptural symbol.

- A cobra uncoils from his lower right forearm, and the crescent moon and a skull are on his crest. He dances within an arch of flames. This dance is called the Dance of Bliss, aananda taandavam.

- The upper right hand holds a small drum shaped like an hourglass that is called a damaru in Sanskrit. A specific hand gesture called ḍamaru-hasta (Sanskrit for "ḍamaru-hand") is used to hold the drum. It symbolizes sound originating creation or the beat of the drum as the passage of time.

- The upper left hand contains Agni or fire, which signifies destruction. The opposing concepts in the upper hands show the counterpoise of creation and destruction or the fire of life.

- The second right hand shows the Abhaya mudra (meaning fearlessness in sanskrit), bestowing protection from both evil and ignorance to those who follow the righteousness of dharmam.

- The second left hand points towards the raised foot which signifies upliftment and liberation. It also points to the left foot with the sign of the elephant which leads the way through the jungle of ignorance.

- The dwarf on which Nataraja dances is the demon Apasmara (muyalaka, as known in Tamil), which symbolises Shiva's victory over ignorance. It also represents the passage of spirit from the divine into material.

- As the Lord of Dance, Nataraja, Shiva performs the tandava, the dance in which the universe is created, maintained, and dissolved. Shiva's long, matted tresses, usually piled up in a knot, loosen during the dance and crash into the heavenly bodies, knocking them off course or destroying them utterly.

- The surrounding flames represent the manifest universe.

- The snake swirling around his waist is Kundalini, the Shakthi or divine force thought to reside within everything. This also parallels the cords of life worn by the Brahmins to represent the second rebirth.

- The stoic face of Shiva represents his neutrality, thus being in balance.

In Tamil Nadu, we find a beautiful image of Ananda Thandava which represents, Soumya (Protector), Roudra (Destructor), Yoga (Philosopher), Nritta (Dancer).

The Nataraja posture is also called "Nadanta", which means no beginning, no end.

There is another interpretation, representing the five koshas. They are:

Annamaya – Physical

Pranamaya – Energy

Manomaya – Emotion

Vignamaya – Unification of conciousness

Anandamaya – Atomic conciousness

The form is obtained by

- combining the navagraha and the 27 points.
- 5 metals – pancha loha representing the 5 elements of the universe.
- Nose – Air, Hair – Water, Face – earth, Brightness – Sky, 3rd eye – Fire.

The idol of Nataraja depends on 2 things, the temple or the place to the proposition of the shiva linga.

The secret of Nataraja idol is, it has 6 triangles and 43 small triangles.

The names of Tandava are:

Ananda, sandhya, Urdhava, Sringara, Tripura, Muni, Samhara, Pralaya, Bhudta, Ugra and Bhujanga.

Fritjof Capra quotes:

"Hundreds of years ago, Indian artists created visual images of dancing Shivas in a beautiful series of bronzes. In our time, physicists have used the most advanced technology to portray the patterns of the cosmic dance. The metaphor of the cosmic dance thus unifies ancient mythology, religious art and modern physics."

We find this written on the 2 Meter statue of Nataraja at CERN, the European Center for Research in Particle Physics in Geneva.

Nataraja Murthy is mystic and holds lot of truth about the universe.

"The dancing foot, the sound of the tinkling bells, the songs that are sung and the varying steps, the form assumed by our Dancing Gurupara – Find out these within yourself, then shall your fetters fall away" – – Thirumular's Thirumanthiram.

CHAPTER 03

BHEDAS

PADA BHEDAS:

Vakshyate padabhedanam lakshnam purwasammatam | |
Mandalaotplavane chaiva bhramari padacharika |
chaturdha padabhedah suh tesham lakshana – muchyate | |

There are four types of movements of feet as described by the ancient scholars. They are 1. Mandala, 2. Utplavana, 3. Bhramaris and 4. Padacharika.

MANDALA BHEDAS:

Sthanakam chayatalidham prenkhana-preritani cha |
pratyalidham swasthikam cha motitam samasuchika | |
parswasuchiti cha dasa mandalaniritaniha |

STHANAKA: Two ardhachandra are to be placed on either side of the waist and stood in samapada.

AYATA: Keeping a distance of vitasti (*approximately 9 Inches*) between two feet and standing in chaturasra. (nearly an Araimandi posture in bharatanatyam/chowka in orissi dance)

ALIDHA: Left foot placed at a distance of 3 vitastis (27 inches) while toes pointing upwards (nearly like naata adavu in Bharatanatyam) and left hand holding shikara and right holding katakamukha.

PRATYALIDHA: The alidha in reverse. right foor placed away and right hand holds shikara and left katakamukha.

PREKHANA: Keep one foot (toes touching the ground and heel not touching the ground) by the side of the heel of other foot and holding kurma hasta.

PRERITA: one foot strikes the ground on the side of the other foot at a distance of 3 vitastis and stand with knees bent, hands holding shikhara near chest and the other holding pataka extended forward.

SWATHIKA: Place the right foot over the other and right hand over the other, keeping the feet and hands crossed (Swasthika)

MOTITHA: standing on the toes and holding tripataka hasta and ground touch by the knees alternatetively.

SAMASUCHI: sit on the ground with toes and knees touching the ground.

PARSWASUCHI: Standing on the toes and one knee on one side touches the ground.

STHANAKA BHEDAS:

padavinyasabhedana sthanakam shadvidham bhavet | |
samapadam chaikapadam nagabhandha statakparam |
aindram cha garudam chaiva brahmasthanamitikramat | |

SAMAPADAM: Standing with feet in sama position.

EKAPADAM: standing on one leg and placing the other on the knees of the first leg.

NAGABHANDHA: Standing posture in which the two legs are interwined and the two hands are likewise twisted with nagabandha hasta.

AINDRA: Standing with one leg bent, raising the knee of the other leg and holding the hands upwards.

GARUDA: At first standing in alidha mandalam, then one knee is placed on the ground while the two hands are held straight.

BRAHMA: If one sits in padmasana.ie. one leg on the knee of the other, and second leg on the knee of the first.

UTPLAVANA BHEDAS:

Athotplavana bhedanam lakshanam parikathyate |
alagam kartari va aswotplavanam motitam tatha | |
krpalagamiti khyatam panchadhotplavanam budhaih |

ALAGOTPLAVANAM: After taking a leap, the two hands holding shikara hasta have to be placed on the either sides of the waist.

UTPLAVANA: After taking a leap stand on the toes, legs crossed, left hand holding kartari is to be placed at the back of the left leg and right holding shikara to be placed right side of the waist.

ASWOTPLAVANAM: Holding tripataka hasta in both hands, take a leap to the front with first leg followed by the second leg and placed alongside.

MOTITA-PLAVANAM: Holding tripataka hasta in both hands and to leap are made as done in kartari but on both side alternately.

KRPALAGOTPLAVANAM: Place the two heels on the waist, ie. touching the hips with the heels, alternatively, and ardhachandra hastas have to be held in between.

BHARAMARI BHEDAS:

Bhramarya lakshnanyatra vakshye lakshana bhedatah |
utplutabhramari chakrabhramari garudabhida | |
tathaikapada bharamari kunchita bhramari tatha |
aksabhramari chaiva tathanga bhramari cha | |
bharamaryah sapta vijneya natyasastra visaradaih |

UTPLUTA: At first, standing in samapada then during a jump the entire body is turned around in the air.

CHAKRA: Holding tripataka hastas in both hands and stamping the ground repeatedly, turn round in circle.

GARUDA: stretching out one feet across the other leg and then knee placed on the ground. after which stretch out the two hands and body turned quickly.

EKAPADA: If one turns round quickly on one foot.

KUNCHITA: turning round, bending the knees.

AKASA: During a jump, if the two feet are stretched apart and then the whole body turned around.

ANGA: Keeping two feet apart at a distance of one vitasti, the body to be turned round and stopped.

CHARI BHEDAS:

Athatra chari bhedanam lakshnam kathyare maya |
adou tu chalanam proktam paschat chamkramanam tatha | |
saranam vegini chaiva kuttanam cha tatahparam |
luthitham lolitham chaiva tato vishmasamcharah | |
charibheda ami astou prokta bharatavedibhih |

CHALANA: Foot is moved from its original place, like walking.

CHAMAKRAMANA: Moving forward like jumping with the outer sides of the feet.

SARANA: Holding pataka hastas, moving forward dragging the heel of one feet with the heel of the other, like a leech.

VEGINI: Holding alapadma and tripataka hasta, move forward in a fast pace on the heels or the toes.

KUTTANA: Striking the ground with the heel or the forepart or the entire sole.

LUTHITA: In the swasthika position of the feet, the ground is struck by the forepart of the foot.

LOLITA: After striking the ground, slightly touch the ground and move.

VISHAMASAMCHARA: When the left foot is encircled by the right foot, and then encircle right foot with the left, move in this manner forward.

CHAPTER 04

REPERTOIRE OF BHARATANATYAM

ALLARIPPU: The term allarippu has its origin from the telugu word 'allarimpu'. It is also known as Mohara or Addi. Allarippu belongs to nritta variety with emphasis on footwork and body movements. The item is divided into 3 phases each performed in 3 degrees of speed – vilambita (slow), madhyama(faster) and druta(fastest). The theme of the item is paying homage to the deity, to the learned and to the common people. The item is very shoty lasting for 3-5 minutes only. Here the dancer begins with Sama paada with her hands held above the head in anjali hasta. It is done is 5 different jathis. Angika abhinaya is given prominence in this item. It is the first item in a bharatanatyam repertoire. The purpose of performing this item first enables the body, limbs to get prepared for performing more difficult items subsequently.

JATHISWARAM: Jathiswaram which is usually presented as the second item in a bharatanatyam repertoire is difficult than allarippu. It belongs to Nritta category. In jathiswaram the rhythmic jathi patterns are interspersed with appropriate swaras. Hence the item is given the name Jathiswaram. Here we use a number of body postures with beautiful rhythmic song accompaniment. It is has no moods or sentiments. It produces an aesthetic pleasure of watching the dancer. Full sequences of adavus in different jathis like tisra, chatustra, khanda, misra and sankeerna are presented in jathiswaram. The song begins with a jathi, then continues with pallavi, anupallavi and charanam. The pallavi is sung many times for which different jathis patterns are choreographed.

SHABDHAM: Shabdham is the third item in a bharatanatyam dance repertoire. In this item the dancer introduces abhinaya for the first time, the abhinaya is composed to simple sahityam which is usually seperated by easy korvais. This item is usually in misra chappu taalam and the mostly in praise of Lord Krishna, though we also find shabdham in praise of Lord Subramanya and Lord Shiva. Generally it tells a synopsis in the first line then giving a description in the later repetitions. After every charanam, a simple sollukattu with simple steps are composed. Each charanam can contain a different story, but essentially deals with same bhavam with one theme. Shabdhams are also referred to as Yasogitams. They have also inherited an islamic influence of repeating the salaamu or Namostute paying respect to almighty or the king) at the end of each line. This pleased the patrons. Initially shabdhams were composed and rendered in one raga, perhaps kambhoji, but it is now a common practice to sing ragamaalika. Eg: "ayar sheriyar" on Lord Krishna, "thillai ambalam" on Lord Shiva.

PADAM: Padam is a musical monologue which resembles a kirtana in structure and propagates the sentiment of love for God through the innumerable aspects of nayika–nayaka bhava. It is a scholarly composition with a perfect blend of sangeeta and sahitya. A musical composition meant especially for dance, that brings out the relationship of naayaka-naayaki (hero-herione) also sometimes, a friend.. The song is so composed as first person telling the story, like either the naayaka or nayaaki or the friend tells the story. Padam has a pallavi, anupallavi and one or two charanams. The first padam in Sanskrit was composed by Vasudeva Kavi who adorned the court of King Sarfoji of Tanjore. Padams involve only abhinaya which is complicated and intricate. There is no footwork in padam. In most cases padams have hero as the paramatma and heroine as jeevatma and the friend as a guide or mentor. Kshetrayya is a very popular composer of padams in telugu. Examples of padams: "theruvil varaano" (in praise of lord nataraja composed by Muttu Tandavar, "Enta chakkani" (on Lord Krishna composed by Kshetrayya)

DEVARNAMA: Devarnama literally means Name of God. Devaranama falls in Natya category. They are compositions of various devotees during the Bhakthi Movement in south india during the 13th to 14th century, especially in Karanataka. The objective was to promote dvaitha philosophy of Madhvacharya through literature. The saints who composed the devaranama were also called Haridasa. These compositions are in praise of the Hindu god Vishnu are called dasara padagalu (compositions of the dasas).These compositions can be more specifically categorized as keertanas,suladis,ugabhogas, and simply padas. They were easy to sing to the accompaniment of a musical instrument and dealt with bhakti (devotion) and the virtues of a pious life. Prominent Hindu philosophers, poets and scholars such as Sripadaraya, Vyasathirtha, Vadirajatirtha, PurandaraDasa and Kanaka dasa, Vadirajatirtha played an important role during this time. The compositions can be broadly classified under one of the following three types:

- *Kavya* or poetic compositions
- *Tatva* or philosophic compositions
- General compositions.

Each Haridasa had a unique *ankita nama*, or pen-name, with which they 'signed' all their compositions. The ankita nama of some of the most well known Haridasas is listed below:

Sripadaraya – Ranga Vittala, Vyasatirtha – Sri Krishna, Vadirajatirtha – Hayavadana, Raghavendratirtha – Dheera venugopala, Purandara dasa – Purandara Vittala, Kanaka dasa – Kaginele adikeshava.

Compositions are in many ragas and generally in Raagamalika and different Thalas. Eg: jaganmohanane Krishna, elli iruvano ranga, baro krishnayya, Bhagyadha lakhmi baramma, indhu yenege govindha.

VARNAM: Varnam is the most enthralling, interesting and a challenging item in a bharatnatyam recital. It is in this piece where in the expertise of the dancer is known.

Varnam was not part of the Sadir Attam till the 18th century. The earliest composer of Varnam is beleived to be Melattur Veerbhadrayya who was in the court of Prataapa Simhaa (1739-1763). The idea of a musical composition with sahitya for all angas was probably suggested by 'Husseni Swarajati' by Veerbhadrayya himself. He is also known to have given a definite shape to Carnatic music. Patchimiriyam Adiyappa, Ramaswami Dikshitulu (1735-1817), Mudduswami Dikshitulu (1775-1835), Shyama Shastri(1763-1827), Ponnaiya and Vadivelu of the Tanjore Quarttette and more are some of the later nattuvanaars who composed Varnams.

There are two kinds of Varnams – one is Pada Varnam and the second is Taana Varnam.

Taana Varanam is mainly intended for musical practice. Much of it is in middle or fast tempo. Though it has sahitya but the sahitya does not have much room for the exposition of rich and variegated abhinaya.

Where as PadaVarnam which is also known as ChaukaVarnam is sung in slow tempo (chaukakaala meaning vilamb or slow tempo) and also give ample scope for abhinaya as well as the nritta.

The perfect synchronisation of Bhava, Raaga and Taala, and equal distribution of nritya and nritta, gives the dancer abundant scope for displaying her rhythmic talents along with rich and variegated abhinaya. It is also a measure of one of the 'Dashapraanas' (the 10 vital characteristics of a good dancer), that is 'ashrama'(endurance), since it is the longest and the most demanding item where in the dancer uses her feet dancing to the Adavu-Jatis, the hands and the hastaas indicating the meaning of the song, while the feeling (inner emotion) is potrayed by the saatvika abhinaya through subtle facial expressions.

Varnam is generally 45 minutes to one hour long item and creates an impression of beauty, grandeur and profundity while depicting the changing moods of love for the hero who is a God. The mood is generally of Shringaara Bhakti – the worship through love.

Stucture of Varnam:

Varnam is divided into two sections:

The 'Purvaranga', that is, the first half comprising pallavi, anupallavi and muktaayi swara, also called as chitta swara with abhinaya being alternated with pure dance steps.

The second half is the 'Urraranga', also called as the 'Ettugada' or 'Charana' comprising ettugada sahitya and ettugada swaraas.

The first half opens with a 'thrikaala termaanam', that is a teermaanam in three kaala (speeds) which is choreographed with complex and graceful adavus, performed to the recital of the 'shollukattu'. Then the pallavi and anupallavi sahitya is alternated with nritta followed by the muktaayi swara and the muktaayi sahitya indicating the end of 'purvaranga'. The pallavi sahitya is rendered once again and then the charana (ettugada) begins with the alternate occurrence of swara and sahitya on one hand and nritta and abhinaya on the other hand. After the last charana swara, the sahitya is rendered again and brought to an appropriate end till the cycle of taala is completed. Eg: " nee indha maayam" in dhanyasi ragam, "roopamu choochi" in thodi ragam, "moham aginen indha velayil" in karaharapriya ragam.

THILLANA: Thillana is a nritta item comprising of beautiful and graceful pure dance steps along with a number of alluringly sculpturesque poses and varied patterns of movements.

Each adavu is executed in Vilambit (slow), Madhya (medium) and Dhrut (fast) kaala (speed) with a meticulous combination of the adavus, resulting in scintillating teermaanams. It ends in Dhrut kaala, thus impressing and spell bounding the audience.

Composed in specific raaga and taala, thillana comprises of pallavi, anupallavi and a sahitya which is in praise of God or the Diety in the temple or the King who has built the temple where the dance used to be performed. Thillana is the last item performed in a bharatanatyam repertoire and is considered as sanctum sanctorium in a dance recital, since it is the final destination that a human being wants to go, to join paramatma. This is the reason, in odissi it is called moksha nritta.

CHAPTER 05

RAGA LAKSHNA

Sangit-Makrand also classifies the ragas according to their gender i.e. Male Ragas, Female Ragas (i.e., Raginis) and Neuter Ragas. According to Narada, the Male Ragas depict emotions of Raudra (anger), Veera (heroic) and Bhayanaka (fearful); the Female Ragas represent sentiments of Shringara (romantic and erotic), Hasya (humorous) and Karuna (pathetic); while the Neuter Ragas represent emotions of Vibhatsa (disgustful), Adbhuta (amazement) and Shanta (peaceful).

Each raga is principally dominated by one of these nine rasas or sentiments, although the performer can also bring out other emotions in a less prominent way. The more closely the notes of a raga conform to the expression of one single idea or emotion, the more overwhelming the effect of the raga.

VASANTHA: Vasantha is a raga in carnatic music. It is a *janya* raga of Suryakantam, the 17th Melekarta ragam. Vasantha is suitable to be sung in evening and is considered an auspicious raga.

Lakshana: *Vasantha* is an asymmetric scale that does not contain *panchamam*. It is called a *vakra audava-shadava* raga,[1] in Carnatic music classification (as it has 5 notes with zig-zag notes in ascending scale and 6 notes in descending scale). Its *ārohaṇa-avarohaṇa* structure is as follows:

- Arohana: S M1 G3 M1 D2 N3 S
- Avarohana: S N3 D2 M1 G3 R1 S

This scale uses the notes *shadjam, shuddha rishabham, antara gandharam, shuddha madhyamam, chathusruthi dhaivatham*and *kakali nishadam.*

Compositions: *Vasantha* has ample scope for alapana. This scale has been used by many composers for compositions in classical music. Here are some popular compositions in *Vasantha.*

- *Ninne kori*, a popular Varnam by Tecchur Singarachari
- *Sitamma Mayamma* by Saint Tyagaraja.
- *Natanam Adinar* by Gopalakrishna Bharathi

THODI: Hanumatodi, more popularly known as **Todi** is a ragam in carnatic music. It is the 8th melakarta ragam (parent scale) in the 72 *melakarta* rāgam system. This is sung very often in concerts. It is known to be a difficult rāgam to perform in owing to its complexity in prayoga (phrases of notes and intonation).

Lakshana: It is the 2nd rāgam in the 2nd *chakra Netra*. The mnemonic name is *Netra-Sri*. The mnemonic phrase is *sa ra gi ma pa dha ni*. Its *ārohaṇa-avarohaṇa* structure is as follows:

- Arohana: S R1 G2 M1 P D1 N2 S
- Avarohana: S N2 D1 P M1 G2 R1 S

This scale uses the notes *shuddha rishabham, sadharana gandharam, shuddha madhyamam, shuddha dhaivatham* and *kaisiki nishadham.* It is a sampoorna ragam – ragam having all 7 *swarams*. A peculiarity of this raga is that it is sung in all lower notes.

Hanumatodi has a quite a few janya rāgams (derived scales) associated with it, of which *Asaveri*, bhupalam, dhanyasi, *Punnagavarali* and *Shuddha Seemandhini* are popular.

Compositions:

- Thaye yashoda by Ottukadu venkatasubhaiah
- Era nai pai – varnam by Patnam Subramania Iyer
- Dasarathi nee runamu by Thyagaraja
- Kamalambike by Muthuswami Dikshitar

KAMBHOJI:

Kambhoji is a *janyam* of *melam* 28, Harikambhoji. It is a typical example of a *janya ragam* that enjoys greater popularity and grandeur, and has a vast number of compositions than the parent scale. (bhairavi is another such example!). kambhoji is an auspicious ragam, so when sung at the commencement of a concert, it generates *"mela kozhuppu"* (proper musical atmosphere). It is a sarva svara gamaka varika rakti ragam, with high emotional impact, which makes a listener very tranquil.

Lakshna:

- **Arohanam:** S R G M P D S
- **Avarohanam:** S N D P M G R S

Besides *Sadjam* and *pancamam*, the notes taken are: *caushruti RiSabham, antara gandharam, shuddha madhyamam, catushruti dhaivatam,* and *kaishiki nisadam.* The note "ni" is omitted in the *Arohanam,* thus making it an Sadava – sampurna (6-7) *ragam.*

Compositions:

- Mandhara dharare by Padala gurum urutti
- Inta Chalamu by Gopala Iyer

- Kailasa nathane by Muthuswami Dikshitar
- Yalane vaani pai (padam) by kshetrayya

SHANKARABHARANAM: Dhīraśankarābharaṇaṃ, commonly known as *Śankarābharaṇaṃ*. It is the 29th melakarta rāga in the 72 *Melakarta* rāga system of Carnatic music. Since this raga has many Gamakās (ornamentations), it is glorified as *"Sarva Gamaka Maṇika Rakti Rāgaṃ"* in telugu.

Its nature is mellifluous and smooth. This rāga offers a large scope for compositions. It is ideal for a melodious, but still laid back majestic presentation.

Lakshana: It is the 5th rāga in the 5th *Chakra Bāṇa*. The mnemonic name is *Bāṇa-Ma*. The mnemonic phrase is *sa ri gu ma pa dhi nu*. Its ārohaṇa-avarohaṇa structure is as follows

- Arohana: S R2 G3 M1 P D2 N3 S
- Avarohana: S N3 D2 P M1 G3 R2 S

The notes in this scale are *shadjam, chatushruti rishabham, antara gandharam, shuddha madhyamam, panchamam, chatushruti dhaivatam* and *Kakali Nishadam*. As it is a *Melakarta* rāga, by definition it is a Sampurna raga (has all seven notes in ascending and descending scale).

Due to the even spacing of *svaras*, many *janya* rāgas can be derived from *Sankarabharaṇaṃ*. It is one of the *melakarta* rāgas that has high number of *Janya* rāgas (derived scales) associated with it.

Many of the *Janya* ragas are very popular on their own, lending themselves to elaboration, interpretation and evoking different moods. Some of them are *Arabhi, Atana, Bilahari, Devagandhari,* Mohanam. Kamsadhavni, *Kadanakutuhalam* and many others.

Compositions:

- Dakshinamurte by Mutthuswami Dikshitar
- Pogadirelo Ranga by Purandara dasa
- Saraja Dala Netri by Syama Sastri
- Chalamela – ata thala Varnam by Swathi Thirunal
- Jana Gana Mana (National Anthem) by Rabindranath Tagore.

MOHANA:

Mohana is a raga in carnatic music, it is an oudhuva ragam meaning it has pentatonic scale. It is a *janya* rāga of Harikambojhi (28th Melakartha Raga). However, there are disputes about Mohanam being the janya of Sankharbharanam also because all the swaras present in the Arohana and Avarohana of Mohanam satisfy both the melakartha ragas listed above. Suitable for singing at all times, but the night time is best suited for this ragam. Ancient name of Mohanam is "regupti" or "raghupati".

Lakshna: *Mohanam* is a symmetric rāga that does not contain *madhyamam* or *nishādham*. Its *ārohaṇa-avarohaṇa* structure is:

- Arohana: S R2 G3 P D2 S
- Avarohana: S D2 P G3 R2 S

Compositions:

- Ninnu kori – Varnam by Poochi Srinivasa Iyengar
- Ranga Nayaka Rajeeva lochana by Sri Purandaradasa
- Nannu Palimpa by Thygaraja
- Kapaali by Papanasam sivan

BHAIRAVI:

Though it is a Sampoorna ragam (scale having all 7 notes), it has two different *dhaivathams* in its scale making it a Bhashanga ragam and hence is not classified as a *Melakarta* rāgam (parent scale).

This is one of the ancient rāgams, said to have been prevalent about 1500 years ago. There are numerous compositions in this rāgam.

Bhairavi is one of the most popular ragas on the concert stage, due to its very wide scope for improvisation. This raga can be elaborated to beautiful effect in all three sthayis, but shines particularly well in the upper madhya and thara sthayis. Bhairavi is also one of the most common ragas in which ragam-thanam-pallavi is rendered, due to the scope for elaboration. It can be sung any time of the day.

Lakshana: It is considered a *janya* of the 20th *melakarta Natabhairavi*. Its *ārohaṇa-avarohaṇa* structure is as follows:

- ārohaṇa: S G2 R2 G2 M1 P D2 N2 S
- avarohaṇa: S N2 D1 P M1 G2 R2 S

The other set of ārohaṇa and avarohaṇa used is:

- ārohaṇa: S R2 G2 M1 P D2 N2 S
- avarohaṇa:S N2 D1 P M1 G2 R2 S

The notes used are *chathusruthi rishabham, sadharana gandharam, shuddha madhyamam,* chathusruthi dhaivatham & shuddha dhaivatham *and* kaishika nishadham. *Note the use of both* dhaivathams, chathusruthi *(D2) in* ārohaṇa *and* shuddha *(D1) in* avarohaṇa.

Compositions:

- Viriboni – Varnam by Pachhimiriam Adiyappa
- Upacharamu by Sri Thygaraja
- Yaro ivar yaro by Arunachala kavi
- Odi barayya by Purandaradasa
- Indu enege govinda by Raghavendra Swami

CHAPTER 06

FOLK DANCE

Indian folk and tribal dances are simple dances, and are performed to express joy and happiness among themselves. Folk and tribal dances are performed for every possible occasion, to celebrate the arrival of seasons, birth of a child, a wedding and festivals. The dances are extremely simple with minimum of steps or movement. The dances burst with verve and vitality. Men and women perform some dances exclusively, while in some performances men and women dance together. On most occasions, the dancers sing themselves, while being accompanied by artists on the instruments. Each form of dance has a specific costume. Most costumes are flamboyant with extensive jewels. While there are numerous ancient folk and tribal dances, many are constantly being improved. The skill and the imagination of the dances influence the performance.

Folk Dances of Karnataka:

They are divided into ritualistic and regional. Regional is again divided into Northern, Southern, Malnadu. There are also divided on the basis of the art form like, dance, music, dance and music, theatre, tribal, mobile and worship oriented folk art.

We shall now discuss the dance oriented folk art of Karnataka:

Ritualistic:

Kunitha – The ritual dances of Karnataka are known as Kunitha. One such dance is the Dollu kunitha, a popular dance form accompanied by singing and the beats of decorated drums. This dance is primarily performed by men from the shepherd or Kuruba caste. The Dollu Kunitha is characterized by vigorous drum beats, quick movements and synchronized group formations.

DOLLU KUNITHA:

1. Dollu kunitha was preserved by Dhewara, oggaligaru and Kuruba caste. Today Nayakar and Jogiyar also perform this.

2. They are worshippers of Bheera Devara.

3. The dance steps are known as:

   - Haasi barisodhu – somersault
   - Huluthu barisodhu – sitting
   - laga hakuvodhu – jumping and turning
   - mandi baditha – knees
   - margaalu baditha – 2-3 sticks
   - gadi chakratha baditha – wheel

4. Other techniques are:

   - ondhu hejje kunitha
   - yeradu hejje kunitha
   - jada hakuvodhu
   - kolu kunitha
   - kudire kunitha

5. It is also called " oddi Valaga" or "Dollu Mela".

6. The costume worn by them is a black blanket at the waist, Thick black thread in a X shape at the shoulder and chest and veebhudhi in the forehead.

7. The dollu is made of Baine, shivene and honne woods. The left side is made of goar skin and right side is made of sheep skin. they also use deer skin.

8. The dimensions of the dollu is usually 1 feet and 8 inches width, 16 feet and 6 inches circumference and 5 feet length.

9. A Pundi Naaru, a thread, is tied around the stick and to the dollu.

10. The stick or kolu is made of people tree which is 2 inches thick and 1 1/4 feet length.

11. Other instruments which can be used while dancing are: dollu, thala, thappidi, nipure, jagate and flute.

12. Music for dollu kunitha is:

   - songs are usually sung which lengthy.
   - which explains the daily routines of life
   - story of halu matha, any social message or theme
   - Ganesh sthuthi
   - devernama
   - beera devera songs
   - dollu sure charitha

13. Dollu kunitha is usually performed during Gowri pooja, marriages, rituals, jatra, processions, bhoomi pournima.

VEERAGASSE AND PURAVANTHIKA:

1. It is prevalent in the northern Karnataka, Gulbarga, dharwad, Shivamogga, Bijapur.

2. The performers are called Puravantharu and the dance is called Puravanthika.

3.　It is performed by Lingayats and Veerashaivaru.

4.　It is ritualistic dance form.

5.　They use a stick named as "Shastra" which is used to pierce through the eyes, tongue and cheeks.

6.　The shastra is 1/4 inch thickness and 3-4 adi length.

7.　They use the shastra pavada technique. There are two in kind:

- Janaveera Shastra

- Phani Shastra

- Gupta

- Khanda

8.　This is performed during marriage ceremony and processions.

9.　If Veergaase is performed, the song or kavya is taken from Puravantharu.

10.　400 – 500 thread is stitched through the stomach and pulled out. Veebhudhi is applied after this.

11.　The end of the performance is called as "kada-kade"

12.　This is performed by professional dancers and it is their livelihood.

13.　This is related to Veeragaase, kasse kunitha, puravanthika, veerabhadhra kunitha.

14.　The costume adorned is:

- white dhoti and saffron jhubba for men.

- Khalifa or coat.

- rhumal – turban in saffron colour

- keertamukha – dollar

- Naga – adorned on both arms in silver skull chain
- anklets
- rudraksha – tied around elbows, wrist and neck
- a bag – raksha jolige
- right side one trishula and left side one shastra pierced in lemon.

15. The intruments used are: samala, kambar, kohala, thala, bronze thala, shahnai.

16. The lyrics of the songs is an extempore.

NANDI DWAJA KUNITHA:

1. This is performed by Shaivaits. Nayakars and Lingayats but now a days Kuruba and oggaligaru also perform this.

2. This is performed during a victory.

3. The places this dance is mostly prevalent are shivamogga, Tumakuru, Davangere, Mysuru, Mandya.

4. The dancer has to follow certain rules in order to perform. They should be fasting and they should not smoke or drink.

5. The nandi dwaja kunitha is made of bronze and is very heavy.

6. They perform:

- one hejje, two hejje and 3 and 4 hejje
- dhoud
- chikku
- thatti
- thirugi hejje

7. Slow pace and fast pace are performed in this dance. First it begins with instrument then dance then Vachana. the cycle continuous again in little fast paced – instrument, dance and vachana.

8. The Kamba is tied with Navaara saree to help in holding with grip.

9. It is generally carried by three people on shoulder, chest, forehead. In Mandya children also carry it on shoulders.

10. The Nandi dwaja Kamba is 20 feet in height.

11. The costume adorned is Dhoti, kurta, waist belt.

12. The instruments used in mandya is Thamate, Tumkur – chamala, karade, nagari, Nagaswaram, Mysore – olaga, thamate, karade.

13. The songs are vachana which explains moral stories, nandi dwaja story, veera bhadra story.

<u>KAMSALE:</u>

1. It is prevalent in the eastern ghats of karnataka.

2. It is in praise of Lord Madheswara, temple mountain also called elu malaya madheswara.

3. Devotees are called devaru gudaru.

4. They get consecration and initiation from this God and become protagonist.

5. They hold cymbols which is made of bronze or brass, that is why it is called kamsale nrutya or the dance of cymbols.

6. They perform various formations.

7. The accompaniments are singing, ektal and damadi or drum.

8. The singer also dances and others follow.

9. The songs are in praise of lord Madheswara.

10. The costume is dhoti which is tied high, a turban and waist belt.

11. The dancers have to lead a truthful, honest and pious life.

YAKSHAGANA:

The coastal Karnataka is a strip between Kasargod and Karwar and between the arabian sea and western ghats including Malnad stretch which is in many ways a geograhical and cultural area that has many peculiarities and specialities. Yakshagana is dance drama of the coastal karnataka. The districts where is mostly prevalent are Uttara kannada, Udupi, dakshina Kannada, Kasargod districts.

1. "Aataa" it is also named in local terms. "yaksha" means exotic tribe (also sometimes known as heavenly people) mentioned in sanskrit, "gana" means music or song.

2. It consists of Himmela – background musicians and Mummela – the dance and dialogue group.

3. The music is based on pre karnataka sangeetha ragas characterised by melodic patterns called mattu and yakshagana thala.

4. Himmela consists of:

   - Bhagavatha – Singer

   - Maddale

   - Harmonium

   - Chande

5. The performance

   - begins with beating of drums at twilight hours and to a fixed compositions called Abbara or Peetike for one hour.

- Pooja for Lord Sri Ganesha is performed

- Then Kodangis or baffoon enacts

- There is loud music by chande and maddala and thala

- In every act there will be Gods, Goddess, Kiratas, Kimpurushas and demons.

- The key characters or Kattu veshas appear after the bhagavatha.

6. The costume is elaborate and colourful. The badagutittu costume is:

- Light wood, mirror work and coloured stones

- Head gear or kirita or pagade, kavacha – chest piece, Buja keerthi, Dabu covered with golden foil, karna kundalas and sonta patti.

- Kachche is red, yellow, orange checks in a big drum shaped.

- Bannada vesha are the monsters

- sthree vesha – uses saree and decorative ornaments

7. Instruments used are:

- Maddale made of jack fruit, kakke, baine or Hunnalu woods

- Thaala made of pancha loha

- Chande is of two types badagu thittu and thenku thittu. The circuar drum head is of processed cow skin.

8. It has evolved from now extinct ghandarva grama musical system which finds mention in Sangeetha Rathnakara as Jakka or Yekkalagaana.

9. Badaguthittu used chende is used. whereas thenku thittu uses kerela maddalam. It is also well known for portraying Rakshas characters with incredible dance steps. There are many dhiginas and spins and several flying dance moves.

10. For characters such as

    • Arjuna, Nakula and Karna multi coloured turbans are used.

    • Cruel characters use big kiritas

    • beautiful characters use same as hero but have red eye, thick moustache and long plait.

    • Divine characters use short turban and yellow dhoti.

11. The common ragas that are usually used in yakshagana are Hamsadhwani, Bhairavi, Atana, Mohana, Neelambari, Shankarabharanam.

12. Early Yakshagana poets include Ajapura Vishnu, Purandaradasa, Parthi Subba, and Nagire Subba, King Kanteerava Narasaraja Wodeyar II (1704–1714) authored 14 Yakshaganas in various languages in the Kannada script. Mummadi krishnaraja Wodeyar (1794–1868) also wrote several Yakshagana prasanga, including Sougandhika Parinaya. Noted poet, Muddana composed several Yakshagana prasangasa, including the very popular Rathnavathi Kalyana.

13. Tenkutitttu: One of the traditional variations, the tenkutittu style, is prevalent in Dakshina Kannada, Kasaragod District, western parts of Coorg (Sampaje), and few areas of Udupi district. The influence of Karnatic Music is apparent in tenkutittu, as evidenced by the type of maddale used and in bhaagavathike. Yakshagana is influenced more by folk art blended with classical dance

aspects. In tenkutittu, three iconic set of colors are used: the Raajabanna, the Kaatbanna, and the Sthreebanna.

The himmela in the tenkutittu style is more cohesive to the entire production. Rhythms of the chande and maddale coupled with the chakrataala and jaagate of the bhaagavatha create an excellent symphonic sound. The dance form in tenkutittu strikes the attention of the audience by 'Dheengina' or 'Guttu'. Performers often do dhiginas (jumping spins in the air) and will continuously spin (sometimes) hundreds of times. Tenkutittu is noted for its incredible dance steps; its high-flying dance moves; and its extravagant rakshasas (demons).

Tenkutittu has remained a popular form and has its own audience outside the coastal areas. The dharmasthala and kateelu durgaparameshwari melas (the two most popular melas) have helped to popularize this form. Several creative tenkutittu plays have been composed by noted scholars, such as Amritha Someshwara.

14. Badagutittu: The Badagutittu style is prevalen North canara (Uttara Kannada District) andhe northern parts of South Canara – from Padubidri to Byndoor, The Badagutittu school of Yakshagana places more emphasis on facial expressions, matugarike (dialogues), and dances appropriate for the character depicted in the episode. It makes use of a typical Karnataka chande.

The Badagutittu style was popularized by Shivaram Karanth's "Yakshagana Mandira," presented at Saligrama Village Dakshina kannada as a shorter more modern form of Yakshagana.

Keremane Shivarama Hegde, the founder of the Yakshagana troupe, Idagunji Mahaganapathi Yakshagana Mandali, is an exponent of the Badagutittu style of Yakshagana. He is also the first Yakshagana artist to receive the Rashtrapati Award from the president of India. He hails from the Honnavar taluk of Uttara Kannada (North Canara) District.

KUMMI:

1. It is one of the most ancient form of folk dance.

2. It has no musical instruments for accompaniment.

3. Only women perform this art form.

4. There are several variations in kummi, they are: poonthatti kummi, deepa kummi, mulaippu kummi, kulavai kummi, kadir kummi.

5. The women dance this in a circle and clapping hands for a catchy tune that they singing while dancing.

6. It is usually performed during temple festivals, pongal, harvest, family functions.

7. The first line of the song is sung by the leader and others follow it.

8. Example for a song is "Kummi adingamma kummi adi".

KOLATA:

1. Kolata is the traditional folk dance of the state of Karnataka located in Southern India on the western coast. Unlike its North Indian counterpart Dandiya Ras, it comes in two forms.

2. First, it is performed with coloured sticks and usually involves both men and women dancing together.

3. Second, very rigorous play of sticks only by men dancing to folk songs. Sticks here are thick and hard to sustain strong play.

4. 'Cheluvayya Cheluvo Tani tandana', 'Kolu kolanna kolu kole' are very popular music for the soft kolata dance of Karnataka.

5. Kolata of men uses 'Indara Gandhi kondavanna', 'Belisalagonda kare beeja' etc. sung vocally along with the dance.

6. Cheluvayya Cheluvo Tani tandana kolata is performed by Kannada Kootas around the world for their Ugadi and Kannada Rajyotsava programmes.

7. There are many types of Kolata, like jade kolata which means plait Kolata. People here jumble themselves holding long dhuppatta.

BHAGAVATA MELA:

Bhagavata mela is a dance drama tradition in Tanjavur is the surviving link between ancient and modern theatre. this cannot be considered as having its origin from any folk play because, the features such as diction, music, dance and abhinaya follow the natya tradition as mentioned in the Bharata's Natya Sastra. with the rulers of south India, the cholla dynasty and the Vijayanagar kings extending their patronage to this kind of performance, the Vaishnavite Bhakthi cult intensified and made way to the blossoming of regular dance drama.

During the latter half of the 16th century A.D., Saint Narayana theertha yogi migrated to Tanjore district and he initiated bhavagathas to perform classical music and dance from bharatanatyam technique which later came to be called as Bhagavatha Mela Natakam. This bhagavatha mela was a commemorative dance drama played yearly in May before the Narasimha temple in the village of Mellathur. The performances celebrate the birthday of Narasimha who is an incarnation of lord Vishnu. A mask of Narasimha and special head dress are used in the performance. the performance. The performance takes place on a platform set before the presiding deity. The Bhagavatar also performs the duties of a stage manager and co-ordinates the entire performance. With this narration of dance drama, Mellathur became the nerve centre of full-fledged classical dance drama. This tradition continued by the followers of Narayana Theertha Yati in later generations. The dance form reached a peak of glory during the time of guru Sri Venkataramana Sastri. He popularised the Melathur dance drama so much that the neighbouring village also started following the traditions. In course of time the tradition fell and it was kept more as a sort of religious formality. Utthukadu Subramaniam Iyer struggled hard to maintain this tradition till the 10s even though Bhagavatha mela artists were satisfied with their profession of agriculture. They cultivated this art form only to keep the tradition but due to social and economic conditions in the village, the actors had to leave the village to seek lively hood in faraway places.

From the time of Vijayanagar rulers Telugu became the court language in south India. the dance dramas were all acted by brahmin Bhagavatars from particular families from generation to another. The female roles were also played by young men, the purpose of art was of two folds, 1st – they were enacted as devotional offerings to God, second – as spiritual and philosophical truth had been sought to be inculcated in the minds of people. The Bhagavata mela play begins with a baffoon – Vidhushaka, followed by a background music who sings the thodai mangalam.

It is embellished with many scintillating sollu kattu, a mask of Ganesh Bhagavan is worn by a young boy and he dances the

Ganesha Kauthuvam before the play actually begins. After this the actual play begins. A curtain is used to introduce the main character. The interpretation songs and speech with hasta mudras and facial expression, synchronisation with rhythmic movements of feet. In this bhagavata mela dance drama, one cannot moss the dominance of dance and rhythm. It is always presented with dignity, grace and refinement. Violent war scenes and killings are not exhibited on the stage. The stage is decorated only with a back and front curtain and minimum use of lights. The makeup and costumes are as far as possible resembles the puranic characters. The dance drama follows vocal music sung by the Bhagavatar and the musical instruments used are thambura, flute, violin, mridanga and thalam. As a classical dance drama, the Bhagavatha mela art form happens to be the only surviving link between the present day classical dance with our ancient theatre tradition.

NAME	PLACE	SPECIALITY	OCCASION	Costume
Ummattaat	Koorg	Designed for ladies	Yugadi, Deepavali,	Red mantle as head gear, jacket and saree.
Kamsale	Mysore	Cymbols are used	Male Mahadeshwara festivals	Dhoti, kurta and cymbols
Nandhi dwaja kunitha	All over Karnataka	18 feet Dwaja is used	Auspicious occasion	Short dhoti, turban
Gombe Aata	Dakshina Karnataka district	Puppets made of cloth, sticks	Any festival or an occasion	The puppets adorn the same style of costume

NAME	PLACE	SPECIALITY	OCCASION	Costume
Keelu Kudure	All over Karnataka	Horse like structure on which the dancer dances	Ceremonies, joyous occasion	Horse structure, head gear
Bootha Nritya	South Canara	Spirit of the ancestors dance	Special occasions	Head gear, bhootha vesha
Dollu Kunitha	Chitradurga, shimoga	The big drum	Any auspicious beginning	Short dhoti, vest belt and dollu.

CHAPTER 07

FAMOUS GURUS AND LEGENDS

Sri Purandaradasa

Purandara Dāsa (1484–1564) is a prominent composer of Dasa Sahithya, a poetic form of the Madhwa philosophy. he is widely referred to as the Pitamaha (lit, "father" or the "grandfather") of carnatic music. He formulated the basic lessons of teaching Carnatic music by structuring graded exercises known as Swaravalis and Alankaras, and at the same time, he introduced the raga mayamalavagowla as the first scale to be learnt by beginners in the field. He also composed Gitas for novice students.

Purandara Dasa addressed social issues in addition to worship in his compositions, a practice emulated by his younger contemporary, Kanakadasa. Purandara Dasa's Carnatic music compositions are mostly in kannada, some are in sanskrit. He signed his compositions with the ankita (pen name), "Purandara Vittala".

He was the only son of Varadappa Nayaka, a wealthy merchant, and Leelavati. He was originally named Srinivasa Nayaka. At age 16 he married Saraswati bai. He lost his parents at age 20, thereby inheriting his father's business of gem stones and pawning. He prospered and became known as navakoti narayana.

A poor man wanted to perform the sacred thread ceremony (upanayana) for his son and came to Srinivasa's wife for money.

Since her husband was a miser, She gave him her nose ring to sell, without the knowledge of her husband and the man sold the nose ring to Srinivasa himself. The miserly Srinavasa lent the man his money. Meanwhile, his wife was worried about what to say to her husband, so she prayed to her favorite deity, who gave her a nose ring just like the one she had just given away. When Srinivasa hurried home, anxious to know if the nose ring was hers, he was bewildered seeing her wear the same one. She confessed what had happened, and he was converted to belief in the virtue of a charitable life. At 30 years of age, he gave away all his wealth to charity and together with his family left his house to lead the life of a wandering minstrel. In his very first song composition, he laments his wasted life of indulgence. It begins with the words 'Ana lae kara' in the shuddha saveri ragam, set to Triputa tala. Srinivasa had his formal initiation at the hands of Vyasatirtha in 1525 when he was about 40 years old, with the name Purandara Dasa bestowed on him. Purandara Dasa traveled extensively through the length and breadth of the Vijayanagara empire in Karnataka, Tirupati, Pandharapura composing and rendering soul stirring songs in praise of god. He spent his last years in Hampi and also sang in Krishnadevaraya's durbar. The mantapa in which he stayed is known as Purandara Dasa Mantapa in Hampi. He died in 1564 at the age of 80. He has composed 4.75 lakh kirtanas. But not more than 700 compositions are available now. His original desire was to compose 5 lakh keerthanas (songs). Being unable to do it in his life, he requested his younger son to complete them. He teaches complete self-surrender and unadulterated love towards Lord Vishnu, the Supreme.

Purandara Dasa systematized the method of teaching Carnatic music which is followed to the present day. He organised a Series of graded lessons such as swaravalis, janti swaras, alankaras, lakshana geetas, prabandhas, ugabhogas, daatu varase, geeta, sooladis and kritis. He also composed a large number of lakshya and lakshana geetas, many of which are sung to this day. His sooladis are musical masterpieces and are the standard for raga lakshana. Scholars attribute the standardization of varna mettus entirely to Purandara Dasa.

Purandara Dasa had great influence on Hindustani music. The foremost Hindustani musician Tansen. His teacher, Swami Haridas was Purandara Dasa's disciple.

Some of his compositions are: Bhagyadha lakshmi baramma, krishna nee begane baaro, kandena govindhana, yeli iruvano ranga.

BALASARASWATHI (1918-1984):

Renowed artist in the field of Bharatanatyam. She was not only famous in India but the entire world for her exemplory performances rendered during her lifetime. She was awarded the Padma Bhushan in 1957 and the Padma Vibhushan in 1977, the third and the second highest civilian honours given by the Government of India. In 1981 she was awarded the Sangeetha kalashikamani award of The Indian Fine Arts Society, Chennai. Dance is a blend of all fine arts. And Balasaraswathi had knowledge of music, sculpture, literature, profound knowledge in dance. this knowledge brough great elegance and beauty to her dance. From generation, in her family, they had been well-versed in dance and music. During late 18th century, Kamakshiammal, the daughter of Rukmini, was a great and popular dancer in the royal court of tanjore. Dhanammal, whose grandmother was kamakshiammal, was a very renowed Veena artists. Jeyyammal was Dhanammal's daughter and she gave birth to Balamma. Sucha a heritage of great art in the family had been an inspiration for the great talent of Balasaraswathi. Balasaraswati created a revolution in traditional music and dance for bharata natyam, a combination of the performance arts of music and dance. She learned music within the family from her infancy, and her rigorous training in dance was begun when she was four under the distinguished dance teacher K. Kandappan Pillai, a member of the famed Thanjavur Nattuvanar family. She did her debut performance at the age of 7 at Amanakshiamma temple in Kanchipuram. When she took up dancing as a profession, she had an opportunity to perform in Chennai which was greatly appreciated. She performed from Allarippu to thillana. Few of her audience were Ariyakudi Ramanuja Iyengar, Kunakkol Master Pakiriya Pillai, Vyadyanath Iyer, Murugapuri Gopalakrishnan. After this revolutionary performance, she came to be known for her impeccable abhinaya. She went on claiming upgradation in Bharatanatyam by rigorous practice under the able guidance of Gouri ammal and Chinnaih Naidu who taught abhinaya. She learnt Kuchipudi from Vedantam lakshmi Narasimha Sastri. Her speech which gained popularity in the year 1975, during the presidential address of Tamil Isai Sangam is " Bharatanatyam is an art oceanic in width and depth. I have taken you a few steps on its shore. I hope the vision you have had of this ocean will inspire you to dive into it and cull its pearl yourself".

Balasaraswathi regards a Bharatanatyam recital like a structured temple: she quotes "we enter the outer tower of alarippu, cross the half-way hall of jatiswaram, then the great hall of sabdam, and enter the holy precinct of the deity in the varnam. This is the place, the space, which gives the most expansive scope to revel in the rhythm and moods and music of the dance. The varnam is the continuum which gives ever-expanding room to the dancer to delight in her self-fulfillment by providing the fullest scope to her own creativity as well as to the tradition of the art. The padams now follow: dancing to the padams one experiences the containment, cool and quiet of entering the sanctum... the expanse and brilliance of the outer corridors disappear... and rhythmic virtuosities of the varnam yield to the soul-stirring music and abhinaya of the padam. Then the tillana breaks into movement like the final burning of incense accompanied by a measure of din and bustle. In conclusion, the devotee takes to his heart the God he has so far glorified. The dancer completes the traditional order by dancing to a simple devotional verse.

Balamma Dynasty

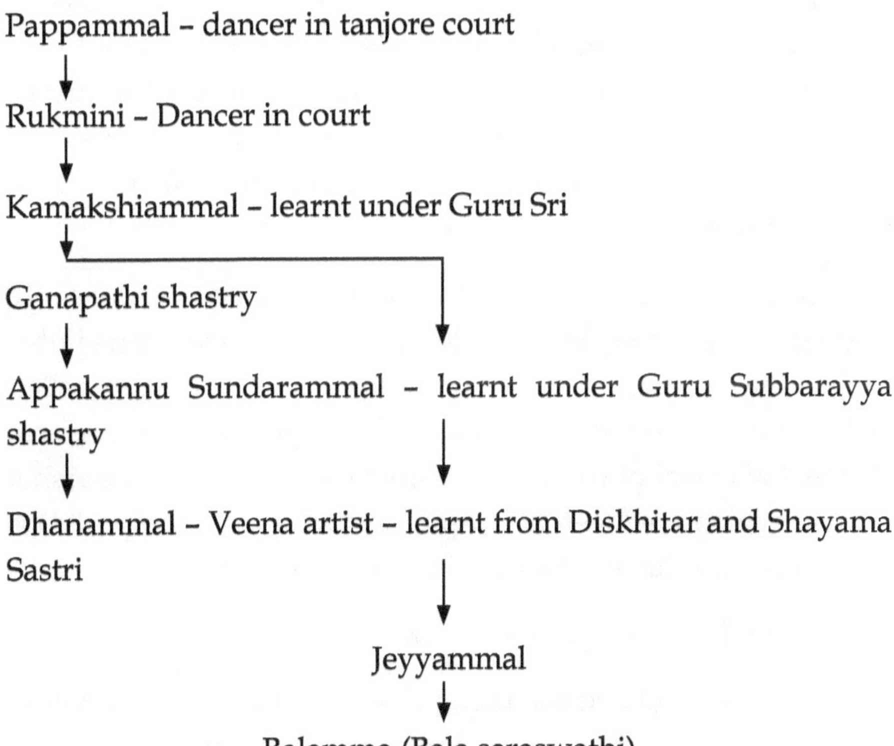

JAYADEVA (12TH CENTURY):

Sri Jayadeva lived during 1200 AD in Orissa. He was a Sanskrit poet who wrote the famous Gita Govinda. Gita Govinda depicts the divine love of Krishna and Radha. He was born in Utkala Brahmin family in a village named Kenduli Sasn in Orissa near Puri. His parents are Bhojdeva and Ramadevi. He received his education in Sanskrit poetry from a place called Kurmapataka. He was married to Padmavathi who was an accomplished dancer. He was also a teaching faculty at Kurmapataka. He excelled in Shastras and Puranas from early childhood.

He was instrumental in popularising dasavatara and tribhangi of Krishna. Guru Granth Sahib has 2 hymns composed by jayadeva because jayadeva's work had profound influence on Guru Nanak. He also institutionalised devadasi system in Oriya temples. Natamandir were built in the temple for dance performances.

The Gita Govinda, the finest Sanskrit poetry comprises 12 chapters, each chapter has 24 divisions called Prabandha. Prabandha contain couplets grouped into eights called Ashtapadi. It is mentioned that Radha is greater than krishna. The text also elaborates the eight moods of Heroine, the Ashta Nayika which has been an inspiration for many compositions and choreographic works in Indian classical dances.

Gita Govinda is a kavya of eminence.

a) It has articulated the erotic love of Krishna and Radha in sublimated idiom giving a mystic and spiritual aura.

b) The opening verse of Gita Givinda is exhilarating and enchanting. The composition of words is unique:

"megair medhuram abharam, vanabhuvas shyamas thamal dhrumair"

c) because of the lucid style of composition jayadeva earned a niche in the heart of all.

d) it is one of the most commented works in Sanskrit poetry.

e) it was translated into many foreign languages also.

f) It is an inspiration to all classical Sanskrit poetic tradition and especially for texts which came after this, apabhrasa and early bhasa poetry.

g) it has descriptive portion and song portion.

The total verses are 386. He led a life of saint during his last days.

KSHETRAYYA (17th CENTURY – 1600-1680):

Kshetrayya was a telugu poet saint. He composed padams and keerthanams. He was born in a village called Muvva, which was in the banks of river Krishna. His original name is Kancharla Goppanna. His pen is "Muvva Gopala". He has written 4000 padams. Krishna was his favourite deity, hence he wrote songs longing for Krishna. He expressed these through the erotic love of Nayaki longing for Nayaka. He had a lot of connection with devadasi, and so he concentrated songs for dance. In his songs, generally anupallavi is sung first and then the pallavi. The madhura Bhakthi is expressed through nayaka and nayaki bhava. His songs are mostly on sringara rasa. After the demolition of devadasi, veena dhanammal and T Brinda popularised his music. Kshetrayya padams have now become an integral part in dance. Some of his songs are: evvade evvade, in Shankarabaranam ragam, Enta chakkani vaada, in abhogi ragam describing svadhina batruka nayika, Aligite bhagya maye maremi in huseeni ragam describing vipralabda nayika, indu endhu vachitiva ra portraying kanditha nayika.

Kshetrayya had once acute stomach pain that couldn't be cured. He then visited many temples praying God. Hence, he got the name Kshetreyya – the one who visited many temples. Finally, when he visited Krishna temple his stomach pain got cured on the grace of God.

KANAKADASA (1509 – 1609):

Kanakadasa was a poet, philosopher, musician and composer from modern Karnataka. He is known for his Kirtanes and Ugabhoga, compositions in the Kannada language for Carnatic music. Like other Haridasas, he used simple Kannada language and native metrical forms for his compositions. **Thimmappa Nayaka** was his original name and he belonged to a chieftain family of Kaginele in Haveri district. He was born to the couple Biregowda and Bachchamma at Baada village. Kanaka Nayaka is from a warrior community and his defeat in the field of battle, directed him to the path of devotion. He belongs to Kurumba Gowda Community; he came to be called **Kanaka Nayaka** as he founded many treasure-troves of gold (*kanaka* means gold in Kannada) during his childhood and never used for self. Kanaka Dasa was well educated and capable of analyzing the society. At a young age he authored poems like Narasimhastotra, Ramadhyana mantra and Mohanatarangini.

Kanakadasa has a special association with Udupi as he was the follower of Vyasaraya Swami ji. On the request of Vyasaraya Swami ji of Vyasaraja Math he had come to Udupi. But it was the era when discrimination on the basis of caste was at its peak. During those days, Thimmappa was not allowed to have darshan of Krishna. When he sang with great devotion, surprisingly, the temple wall fell down and the deity of Lord Krishna turned around and there was a crack in the outer walls of the temple through which Thimmappa was able to see Bhagavan. Since then, the Krishna deity has been facing west even though the main entrance has been facing east and this has remained a mystery ever since.

His writing started showing his innovativeness in using day-to-day activities of common man. For e.g. *Ramadhanya Charite* talks about the conflicts between rich and poor classes where he uses Ramadhanya ragi to synonymously represent poor and rich. He joined Haridasa movement and became a follower of Vyasaraja who named him as Kanakadasa. His poems and krithi deal with many aspects of life and expose the futility of external rituals. The deity he worshiped was Adhikeshava of Kaginele, presently in Haveri district of Karanataka. Out of the many of his compositions, about 240 are available today. All his compositions end with mudra (signature/pen name) *Kaginele Adhikeshava*. Some of his major works are: Nalacharitre (Story of Nala)

Haribhaktisara (crux of Krishna devotion)

Nrisimhastava (compositions in praise of Lord Narasimha)

Ramadhanyacharite (story of ragi millet) and an epic

Mohanatarangini (Krishna-river).

In addition to being a poet he worked as a social reformer. He effectively used music to convey his philosophy. He lived at Tirupathi in his last days. He is one of the greatest musician, composer, poet, social reformer, philosopher and saints that India has ever seen.

CHAPTER 08

DEVATHA HASTAS

BRAHMA:

'Brahmashchaturo vame hansasyo dakshine kare'

Bhagawan Brahma is the creator. He is born out of the Naabhi (navel) of Bhagawan Vishnu. He has four faces from which the four vedas are born. He is depicted as sitting on the lotus and riding on the swan. His consort is Devi Saraswathi, the goddess of wisdom.

Bhagawan Brahma is represented with chathura in the left hand, which denotes the Vedas. Hamasyo is held on the right hand denoting wisdom.

SHIVA:

'Shambovarmay mrugashirshas tripatakastu dakshina'

Bhagawan Shiva is the destructor. In the form of Nataraja, he is the cosmic dancer. He has a third eye which when opened creates great destruction. He can dance seven types of thandavam which is performed on different occasions. River ganga flows onto the earth from his head, a crescent moon is on the jatajootam of the shiva, he ties the tiger skin and has snakes and kapala as his ornaments. His body is ash smeared and he is also known as neelakanta. He rides on Nandi and his consort of Parvathi Devi.

Bhagawan Shiva is denoted by holding mrigashirsha hasta on the left hand and tripataka hasta on the right hand.

VISHNU:

'Hastabhyam tripakastu vishnuhastaha kirititaha'

Bhagawan Vishnu is the protector of the universe. He has many avataras, he holds the shanku and chakra, gadha. The ten avatara of Vishnu are matya, kurma, varaha, narasimha, vamana, parashurama, rama, Krishna, bhudha and kalki. He reclines on the adisesha in the milky ocean. His consort is Lakshmi devi. He rides the giant bird, garuda.

He is denoted by holding tripataka hasta on both the hands.

SARASWATHI:

*'suchi krute dakshinecha vame chasamkrutau chamsamakrutau
Kapittyakepey bhaatayah kara syaditi sammattaha'*

Saraswathi devi is represented by holding the suchi hasta on the right hand near

the chest and kapitha hasta on left hand near shoulder level.

PARVATHI:

*'Udhvardaha prasutavardhachandrakhyo vamadakshinau
Abhayo varadachaiva parvaryaha karaeritaha'*

Parvathi Devi is portrayed by holding the ardhachandra hasta on both the hands, one hand pointing upwards and the other pointing downwards, denoting Abhaya and varada hastas.

LAKSHMI:

'amsopakanthe hasta bhyam kapityashtu shriyaha karaha'

Lakshmi devi is represented by holding kapitha on both the hands near the shoulder level.

GANESHA:

'urogatabhyayam hastabhyam kapitho vignaratkaraha'

Bhagawan Ganesha is represented by holding kapitha hasta on both the hands, one facing down and the other up, near the stomach.

SHAMNUKHA:

'vame kare trishulashchya shikaro dakshine kare
Urdhvam gate shamnukhasya hastaha syaditi kirtitaha'

Bhagawan Shanmukha or Kartikeya is represented by holding the trishula hasta on the left hand near the thigh and shikara hasta on the right hand near the shoulder.

MANMATHA:

'vame karetu shikarau dakshine katakamukhaha
Manmatasya karaha natyasastrartha kovadaihi'

Manmatha is represented by holding katakamukha on the right hand and shikara hasta on the left hand, both near the chest.

INDRA:

'Tripatakscha swasthikascha shikrhastaha prakirthitah'

Bhagawan Indra is portrayed by holding triptaka hasta on both the hands by crossing it abive the head.

AGNI:

'tripatako dakshinetu vame kangulahastaha
Agni hastah sa vigneyo natyashastra visharadaihi'

By holding the Kangula hasta on the left hand and tripataka on the right hand, Agni deva is denoted.

VARUNA:

'patako dakshine vamay shikaro varunaha karaha'

Varuna deva is represented by holding pataka hasta in the right hand and shikara hasta in the left hand.

VAYU:

'aralo dakshine haste vaame chaardhapatakika
Dhruta chet vaayudevasya kara ityabhideeyate'

Vayu deva is portrayed by holding the Arala hasta in the right hand and Ardhapataka hasta in the left hand.

KUBERA:

'vaame padmam dakshine tu gadaa yakshapateh karah'

The alapadma is held on the right hand and mushti on the left hand, this denoted the Yaksha raja, Kubera.

YAMA:

'vame paasham dakshine tu soochi yama karaha smritaha'

Yama raja is portrayed as holding pasha hasta on the left side and then hold the soochi hasta on the right hand.

NIRUTI:

'khatva cha shakatas chiava keertitou nirutteh karaha'

Nirutti is represented by holding the shakata hasta on the right side and then holding the khatva hasta on the left hand.

CHAPTER 09

CHATHURVIDA ABHINAYA

"angiko vachikah tathva aharaya sattviko – aparah |
Chaturdhabhinaya tatra cha angiko – angaih nidarsitah | |
Vachavirachitah kavya nataka adhishu vachikah |
Aharyoharakeyura veshadibhiralamkrtah | |
Sattvikah sattvikaih bhavaih bhava jnena vibhavitah | |"

Abhinaya or Expressions is one of the most important factors in Indian dance. It literally means the representation or exposition of a certain theme. It is derived from Sanskrit **Abhi – to or towards, Ni – roots** or leading to. Bharata explains abhinaya as exhibiting the meaning of that which is depicted.

There are 4 aspects of abhinaya, which is also described in the sloka *"Angikam* bhuvanam yasya *Vachikam* sarva varmayam *Aharyam* Chandra tharadhi tham namaha *Sathvikam* shivam"

They are: Angika, Vachika, Aharya and Sathivika.

Angika Abhinaya – It is the language of expression through the medium of the body (sharira), the face (mukha) and movement (chesta). The angas are the major limbs, Pratangas and Upangas are the minor limbs. The main limbs when in movement will automatically utilise the minor limbs.

Anga – Anga consists of head, hands, chest, wrists and feet. There are 6 angas. Some authors also include neck as an anga.

Pratanga – This consists of shoulders, arms, back, thigh, belly. Others add 3 more such as waist, elbows and knees.

Upanga – This consists of eyes, eyesbrows, eyeball, cheek, nose, jaws, lips, teeth, tongue, chin are the upangas of the face alone. Heels, ankles, toes and fingers are few other upangas.

<u>Vachika Abhinaya:</u> The sacred treaties (Sastra) are formed from words. This verifies there is nothing beyond words. In classical dance, the singer gives expression to the words of song while the dancer interprets the meaning. This understanding between the musician and the dancer is of extreme importance. Apart from melodious voice of the singer, clarity is necessary in music and movements of dance, so that the audience can enjoy and understand each and every word that the dancer interprets. In some dance forms the dancer recites the verses on the stage aloud. Vachika is a vital factor as this makes understanding of the expressions easier. Vachika Abhinaya is extensively used in Drama and dialogue oriented art forms.

<u>Aharya Abhinaya:</u> This abhinaya is done through make-up and costume. In dance and drama, as soon as the character appears on the stage the physical form and figure is first noticed, then the words and then the acting is recognised. Hence Aharya abhinaya is significant for an immediate impression and a first expression.

The activity behind the curtain is broadly divided into 4 main aspects:

a) Pushta or set construction

b) Anga rachana or making up the face and body with paint etc.

c) Alankara or decoration

d) Sanjeeva or live presentation of animal or birds etc.

Pushta: Various objects are grouped together and modelled to represent mountain, vehicles, flag staff etc for creating necessary illusion on the stage. This can be achieved by three processes:

- Sandhima – Preperation of the necessary shapes and forms like pulp mats, bamboos, leather, cloth etc.

- Vyaajima – Animation of the objects by means of wires, servers and ropes.

- Veeshitima – Creation of objects with drapery.

<u>Anga Rachana:</u> Painting the face and the body with colours. There are three major colours and combination of major colours bring minor colours. Bharata described elaborately the colours and characteristics of individuals living in various parts of the world. Eg: faces with beard and without, clean shaven, rusty etc. The head gear representing the Gods and the kings, for others, turbans, wings etc. Hair styles for men and women are also explained well by Bharata.

<u>Alankara:</u> Decoration of the various parts of the body with appropriate flowers, jewels and clothes are known as alankara. Again, these three main aspects are sub divided.

Bharata explains in detail about the ornaments and costume for men and women. Heavy and realistic jewellery should not be worn on the stage as it hinders free expression.

Flowers are divided into 5 types:

- Veeshitima or bouquets

- Vitasta – garlands

- Sanghaatya – garlands concealing the 5 stalks

- Grandhima – making garlands with bouquets

- Praalambita – open garlands reaching the knees

Jewellery is divided into 4 types:

- Aaveedhya – ear ornaments
- Bhandhaneeya – waist bands
- Aaloopya – Necklace
- Prashkeepya – Ankelts

Costume is divided into 3 types:

- Sudha – white
- Rakta – coloured
- Vichitra – multi coloured

Sanjeeva: The entry of living creature into the stage is called Sanjeeva. This is divided into 3 types:

- The 4 legged eg – animals
- The 2 legged eg – birds and humans
- The non legged – serpents

Saathvika Abhinaya: An actor might not have experienced what he/she is enacting on stage yet the actor has to portray or convey in a way that the audience understand it. That emotion which is felt, involuntarily or automatically exhibits itself outwardly, like tears or fainting. The word sattvika is endowed with the quality of sattva or purity. Sathvika abhinaya is depicting or acting a state of mind which has been caused by natural emotion. In kathakali and Kuttiyattam this abhinaya has been developed to the fullest. They hold a middle place between the sthayi bhavas and vyabhichari bhavas. Saathvika abhinaya is of 8 types:

- Stambha: It is caused by joy, fear, disease, surprise, anger. It is represented by inactivity or immobility.

- Sveda: It is caused by anger, weariness, heat, exhaustion. It is depicted by perspiration and actions showing desire for breeze.

- Romancha: It is caused by touch, surprise, cold, extreme bliss. It is depicted by hair standing on the body.

- Swarabhedha: It is extreme anger, fever, intoxication. It is depicted by broken or choking face.

- Vepathu: It is caused by fear, cold, sudden emotion. It is depicted by rubbing or shaking.

- Varanya: It is caused by sudden news, fatigue. It is depicted by changing the colour of face or putting pressure on limbs or weakness of limbs.

- Ashru: It is caused by happiness, smoke, yawning, sorrow. It is depicted by shedding tears.

- Pralaya: It is caused by intoxication, slips, injury, sudden movement outside, tiredness. It is depicted by falling on the floor.

Rasa and Bhava:

"Vibhava anubhava vyabhichari bhava samyogaat rasa nishpathih"

It is the most important concept in Indian fine arts.

Vibhava → Anubhava → Vyabhichari bhava → Sthayi bhava → Rasa

Reason → Reaction → Passing state of mind/actions → Permanent state of mind → Rasa/Essence.

Eg:1. Fear: Seeing Snake → Opening eyes → worry/death → bhayya → Bhayanaka.

2. Love: Seeing God → gentle smile → emotional/joy → Rati → Sringara.

Bhava: The state of mind (chittavikara). The inner feeling which is felt is called bhava. According to Dhananjaya (author of dasarupaka) bhava means expressing the accumulated feelings in a unit manner. According to Natya sastra bhava means that which embodies words, anga and sattva. There are three types:

1. Sthayi bhava – 8
2. Sanchari bhava – 33
3. Satthivika bhava – 8 = **Total = 49**

Vibhava: It is the reason or motive for bhava. Hence the origin bhava begins from vibhava. There are two kinds:

1. Udhippana – Supportive reason
2. Alambana – Main reason

Anubhava: It is the result or reaction of the bhava that has occurred. That which is felt afterwards is called anubhava. If the vibhava is the source of bhava, anubhva makes the bhava stand out prominently.

Sthayi Bhava: Stable or permanent state of mind. There are 8 kinds. The sthayi bhava remains constant from the beginning until the end.

Vyabhichari bhava: It means they come and go in aesthetic delight. That which appears and disappears according to the need of the act. They are 33 in number.

Sathivika Bhava: It is the potential state of mind. Sattva is something which arrives only when mind is calm and clear. They are 8 kinds:

1. Stamba – Still
2. Svedha – Sweating
3. Romancha – Thrill
4. Svarabedha – Trembling
5. Vepathu – Shivering
6. Vyvarya – Change in colour
7. Pralaya – Unconsciousness
8. Ashru – Tears

QUESTION AND ANSWERS

QUESTION PAPER – CLASS TEST I

PORTIONS:

INDIAN CLASSICAL DANCES, CHATHURVIDHA ABHINAYA, MUSICAL INSTRUMENTS

I. ANSWER ANY FIVE 5 * 8 = 40

1. Write the meaning of the term Bharata. Write about Bharatanatyam.

2. What are the types of abhinaya? Explain aharya in detail.

3. What are the classical dance forms of Kerala? Explain.

4. What is the name of the jewellery worn by Orissi dancers? Explain.

5. Write the names of dances styles of Manipuri? Explain.

6. What are the types of musical instruments?

7. Explain the Sathivika Abhinaya.

8. Explain Avanadha and Thatha musical instruments.

II. FILL IN THE BLANKS 5 *1 = 5

1. ___________ brought the renaissance of Manipuri.

2. Vachika abhinaya is ___________ of expression.

3. Tanjore brothers were appointed in the courts of ___________.

4. Bhama kalapam is popular dance item of ___________.

5. Harmonium is a ___________ instrument.

III. ANSWER ANY 6 QUESTIONS 6 * 5 = 30

1. Explain in short about Manipur and Sattriya classical dance forms of India.

2. Write about a guru in Bharatanatyam mention the place and style.

3. Write how the chathurvidha abhinaya can be used in a Bharatanatyam performance.

4. Write the about Thala in Carnatic classical form.

5. Write the angas of the thala, with example.

6. Write about angika abhinaya.

7. Write about bhama kalapam in kuchipudi.

IV. ANSWER THE FOLLOWING 10 * 2 = 20

1. Write the repertoire of Bharatanatyam.

2. Write about vachika abhinaya.

3. What are the instruments used in a kuchipudi performance.

4. Quote the shloka that describes all four abhinayas of Bhagawan shiva.

5. Write about Tarangam.

6. How is aharya abhinaya important in Bharatanatyam. Explain.

7. Explain the nishabdha and shashabdha kriyas.

8. Explain the Dhruva, khanda jaathi thalam.

9. Why is Natya Veda called as Panchama veda?

10. Write about the Nepaathya used in Kathakali.

V. MATCH THE FOLLOWING 5 * 1 = 5

1.	Sathvika	a) Padam
2.	Jumpa	b) 3
3.	Tisra	c) inner feeling
4.	Gotipua	d) 1U0
5.	Indhu endhu vachithivi	e) Orissi

QUESTION PAPER – CLASS TEST II

PORTIONS

Terminologies, Glory of Nataraja and Life history of legends

I. ANSWER ANY FIVE 5 * 8 = 40

1. Write about the spirituality of idol of Nataraja.

2. What is Nattuvangam?

3. Write the difference between Jathi, korvai and theermana.

4. What is Deha Sthana?

5. Who was Kshetragna?

6. Write a note on Tanjore brothers.

7. Explain the life history of Balasaraswathi.

II. FILL IN THE BLANKS 5 *1 = 5

1. _________ is the base for Nrutta.

2. Hastha pranas are _________ in number.

3. Mukthayi is always presented _________.

4. Nataraja dance represents the _________ kriyas.

5. _________ is the Pitha Maha of music.

III. ANSWER ANY 6 QUESTIONS 6 * 5 = 30

1. Write life history of kanaka dasa briefly.

2. Explain the Sapta Tandavam.

3. Explain the desi and margi dances.

4. Explain the rechaka.

5. Explain write the dasavidha advaus.

6. What is generally used to make Ntaraja idol and name a few temple where one can find the deity of Nataraja.

IV. ANSWER THE FOLLOWING 10 * 2 = 20

1. What is Nritta Hasta?

2. Explain the term Shollukattu.

3. Why is Nataraja deity regarded as Cosmic dancer?

4. Which is the place, where one can one find the idol of Nataraja on the outside of the building?

5. Why are the compositions of Dasa named as Dasa Sahitya?

6. Write a short note on Kalyani Kutti amma.

7. What are the compositions of Jayadeva called?

8. Write a note on Venkatalakshmma?

9. What is a Bhrata?

10. Why is rangapravesha the first milestone for a dancer?

V. MATCH THE FOLLOWING 5 * 1 = 5

1. Natya   a) Thandava

2. trikala   b) venkatalakshmma

3. Nrutya   c) Abhinaya

4. Jatti thayamma   d) Speed

5. Samhara   e) Pure dance and Expressions

QUESTION PAPER – CLASS TEST III

PORTIONS:

Hasta Mudras, Taala prakaranam, Raaga Lakshanam, Aharya Abhinaya

I. ANSWER THE FIVE 5 * 8 = 40

1. What is the viniyoga and lakshana of any 5 hastamudras.

2. Write about the thala system of Carnatic music.

3. Give the raga lakshnama of kamaas, kaanada, Mohana, anandabhairavi.

4. Write about aharaya abhinaya.

5. Write in detail raagam, thalam and how it is vital for dance.

II. FILL IN THE BLANKS 5 *1 = 5

1. Nritta hastas are __________ in number.

2. Lake, sea, river are usages of __________ hasta.

3. Thunda darshane is a viniyoga of __________ hasta.

4. 1011 is a anga of __________ thalam.

5. Vyajima is __________ type of abhinaya.

III. ANSWER THE QUESTIONS 6 * 5 = 30

1. Write the importance of Mudras in dance.

2. How is the jewellery and make up of Bharatnatyam dance?

3. Explain jumpa thalam khanda jathi, ata thalam sankeerna jathi, triputa thala chathusra jathi, matya thalam misra jathi, roopaka thalam trisra jathi thalam.

4. Explain the lakshana of shankarabharanam, vasantha, thodi.

5. Explain the lakshnas of any five samyutha hastas.

6. What is the importance of aharya abhinaya in Bharatanatyam.

IV. ANSWER THE FOLLOWING 10 * 2 = 20

1. What are nritta hastas?

2. Explain bhairavi raga.

3. Explain briefly about the ancient aharya abhinaya used in Bharatanatyam.

4. How are the ragas classified in Carnatic music?

5. What are the sooladhi sapta thalas?

6. What is shashabdha kriya and nishabdha kriya?

7. What are the usages of mayura and mrigasheersha hastas?

8. How do you define a svara?

9. Explain the lakshana of Kalyani.

10. What is hasta prachara?

V. MATCH THE FOLLOWING 5 * 1 = 5

1. Asamyutha hasta   a) Karaharapriya

2. alapadma   b) Live beings

3. sanjeeva   c) Mirror

4. 0   d) 28

5. Kaanada   e) anudhruta

QUESTION PAPER – CLASS TEST IV

PORTIONS:

Paadabhedas, repertoire of Bharatanatyam, folk dances of Karnataka, hastamudra (part2)

I. ANSWER THE FIVE 5 * 8 = 40

1. What are the paada bhedas? Give its classification and sloka.

2. Write about varnam and thillana.

3. Write about Dollu Kunitha.

4. What is the nritta hasta, write its sloka.

5. Write about the devatha hastas.

II. FILL IN THE BLANKS 5 *1 = 5

1. Chari is _________ movement of the body.

2. Devernama is a _________ item.

3. Nandi Dwaja Kamba is made of _________.

4. Hasta kshetra means _________.

5. Devatha hasta are _________ in number.

III. ANSWER THE QUESTIONS 6 * 5 = 30

1. Write about kolata and kamsale.

2. What is utplavana bhedas.

3. Write the differences between shabdam and varnam.

4. Write about Yakshagana.

5. Write about bhagavatha mela.

6. What is the importance of Bharatnatyam margam?

IV. ANSWER THE FOLLOWING 10 * 2 = 20

1. Write the sloka for hasta kshetra.
2. Write what is kummi.
3. What is the sloka of sthanka bhedas?
4. What is the difference between hasta kshetra and hasta prachara.
5. What is allarippu?
6. What is the sloka of brhamari bhedas?
7. What is the importance of folk art forms?
8. Write the difference between padam and javali.
9. What is the sloka of mandala bhedas.
10. Write about the dehasthana.

V. MATCH THE FOLLOWING 5 * 1 = 5

1. Nritta hasta   a) 10
2. Devatha Hasta   b) 13
3. Asamyutha   c) 16
4. Samyutha   d) 28
5. Mandala bhedas   e) 24

SAMPLE QUESTION PAPERS

PAPER 1

I. Answer any five of the following questions 5 * 8 = 40

1. Write the shlokas of asamyutha and hasta according to abhinaya Darpana.

2. Explain the hexagonal pattern of lord Nataraja.

3. Name chaturvidha abhinaya and briefly explain angika abhinaya and vachikabhinaya.

4. Explain the characteristics of the following nrithya bandhas.

   a) Shabdham

   b) Thillana

5. Write a short note on the given terminologies.

   a) Tandava

   b) Lasya

6. Write the shlokas for given devata hastas.

   a) Shambhu

   b) Indra

   c) Lakshmi

   d) Vayu

7. Explain the six types of 'sthanaka mandala'

8. Explain the mohiniattam art form.

II. Answer any six of the following questions 6 * 5 = 30

1. Write the usages of the following hand gestures with shlokas.

   a) Mayura hasta

   b) Pushpaputa hasta

2. Write a note on Javali.

3. What is Mukthaya? Explain.

4. What is Rangapravesha? Explain.

5. What is Adavu? Explain the four features of adavus.

6. Write the differences between nruthya and natya.

7. What is the contribution of Karnataka in the development of Bharatanatyam?

8. Explain the types of Bhramari.

III. Answer the following in two or three sentences. 10 * 2 = 20

1. Define shollukattu.

2. 'Bhakaro Bhava Samyutho', complete the following shloka.

3. What are the five actions (panchakriye) of Ananda tandava shiva?

4. Define desi and margi.

5. What is anga Shuddhi?

6. Which are the types of lasya? Define them.

7. Write the uses of arala hasta and shukathunda hasta along with shloka.

8. What is jathi?

9. What is Sathvika Abhinaya?

10. Name the Nrutha hasta according to Abhinaya Darpana.

IV. Write the corresponding word for the first two words as given in the example. 5 *1 = 5

Natyasastra: Bharatamuni:: Lasyaranjana: Simhabhupala

1. Kuberahasta:Devata hasta:: Ardharechita: _________

2. Brahmasthana: Sthanakamandala:: Kripalaga: _________

3. Kartharimukha: Asamyutha hasta:: Karthari Swasthika: _________

4. Expression through body movements: Angika abhinaya:: Verbal expressions: _________

5. Allarippu: Invocatory dance:: Thillana: _________

V. Match the Following 5 * 1 = 5

1. Adavallavan		a) Muyyalaga
2. Tandava		b) Bharata
3. Lasya		c) Nataraja
4. Natyasastra		d) Tandumuni
5. Short Demon		e) Sarangadeva
		f) Ushe

PAPER 2

I. Answer any five of the following 5 * 8 = 40

1. Write the characteristics of vasantha and thodi ragam.

2. Write a brief history of poet jayadeva.

3. Describe the costume and jewellery used in Bharatanatyam.

4. Write the difference between jade kolata and kummi kolata.

5. Write about the contribution of Tanjore quartet to the field of Bharatanatyam.

6.   Explain the saptha thalas along with signs.

7.   Write the similarities and differences between bhagavatha mela and Kuchipudi.

8.   Write a short note on any two janapada dance of Karnataka.

II. Answer any Six of the following. 6 * 5 = 30

1.   Write a short note on Koravanji.

2.   Write a short note on Suggi Kunitha.

3.   Write the contribution of Purandaradasa to the field of music.

4.   Write the costumes used in Mohiniattam dance.

5.   Explain the history and Gharana styles of Kathak.

6.   Write a note on Ummathat folk dance.

7.   Write a short note on Yakshagana.

III. Answer any ten of the following. 10 * 2 = 20

1.   Write about Rasa.

2.   What is Janka raga.

3.   Name the regional dances of Kodagu.

4.   Write arohana and avarohana of kannada raga.

5.   Write about maharis.

6.   Name any 2 instruments used for shruti in the olden days.

7.   What is janya raga?

8.   Khanda jathi atta thalam and tisra jathi Dhruva thala – write the anga for these two.

9.   Who is Kanaka Dasa and what is his pen name.

10. Write about the learning process of Odissi dance in 3 sentences.

11. Write the names of 5 colours which is mainly used in Kathakali.

12. Define Natya.

IV. Fill in the Blanks 5 *1 = 5

1. Pralokita comes under _________ bheda.

2. Nrutya adi devete _________.

3. In _________ abhinaya, spirituality is prominent.

4. Writer of lasya Ranjana _________.

5. Pen name of Purandara Dasa is _________.

V. Correct the following 5 * 1 = 5

1. Yakshagana is a classical dance.

2. Dhruvathala is 101

3. Name of the writer of Geeta Govinda is Kshetragna.

4. Kathak is a classical dance of tamil nadu.

5. Varna is important dance of Bharatanatyam.

PAPER 1 (PRACTICAL)

1. Show the students the below mentioned hastas and ask for viniyogas. 6 *5 = 30

   a) Tripataka

   b) Kartari mukha

   c) Kapota

   d) Anjali

   e) Mayura

   f) Ardhachandra

   g) Dola

   h) Kapitha

2. Answer any five devatha hastas with shloka. 5 *2 = 10

3. Sing a tana varana. 5

4. Khanda jathi allarippu – recite with thala. 10

5. Sing the first two jathis of Pada Varana and its Chittai Swaram. 15

6. Sing the shabdam. Mention its raga, thala, bhava Artha and composer. 10

7. Sing a jaavali. Mention its raga, thala, composer. 10

8. Sing a thillana. Mention its raga, thala and composer. 10

PAPER 2 (PRACTICAL)

MAX MARKS = 150

1. Students to show the below yoga asana. 4 * 5 = 20

   a) Padma asana

   b) Bhujanga asana

   c) Manduka asana

   d) Trikona asana

- Students to show the adavus mentioned below in three speeds. 6 * 5 = 30

   a) Naatu adavu – misra jaathi

   b) Egaru thattu (kudith thattu) – khanda jaathi

   c) Jaaru adavu – trisra jaathi

   d) Mukthayi adavu – sankeerna jaathi

   e) Rangakramana adavu – chaturasra jaathi

   f) Mettu adavu – tisra jaathi

- Do Allarippu.

   a) First half in one jaathi and second half in another jaathi.   20

   b) Describe what is Alarippu.   10

- Do jathiswara.

   a) Perform jathiswaram first half in one raga and second half in another raga.   20

   b) Describe what is jathiswaram.   10

- Describe what is Kauthuvam.   10

- Shabdam –

    a) Describe what is shabdam. Mention its raga, thala, composer and bhava aratha.   **10**

    b) Perform any shabdam.   **20**

PAPER 3 (PRACTICAL)

MAX MARKS = 150

1. a) Perform the Pada Varana from Trikala to Pallavi and then the chittai swaram.   **30**

    b) Mention its raga, thala, composer and bhava Artha. **10**

2. a) Perform kshetragna padam from Pallavi to charanam. Mention its raga, thala, composer and bhava Artha.   **20**

    b) Perform the charanam of another padam. Mention its raga, thala, composer and bhava Artha.   **10**

3. Perform one Javali completely. Mention its raga, thala, composer and bhava Artha.   **30**

4. Perform to any dance number of your choice. Mention its raga, thala, composer and bhava Artha.   **15**

5. Perform the Adi thala thillana for its first half and another thillana for its second half. Mention its raga, thala, composer and bhava Artha.   **25**

ABOUT THE AUTHOR

Dr. Meghna Venkat is a Bharatanatyam artist. Her dissertation, "The Impact of Rasa Sutra on Bharatanatyam," was the subject of her doctorate in dance. She is an empanelled artist of The Ministry of Culture, Govt of India. She is a graded artist of Doordarshan. Selected for lectureship under UGC-NET Central Government examination. She is a recipient of awards like Natya Chemmal, Nrutya Kowmudhi, Nritya Shiromani to mention a few. She has established 'Nritya Nadam Vidhyalaya', a school imparting training in Fine Arts.

She conducts a binniel festival named Aikyam – an International Thematic Dance festival. She has also conducted an Online Arts Initiative named, Bridge the Gap initiative, during the first wave of the pandemic, which was first of its kind. Through the initiative she collected Rs. 1.85 lakhs and donated the entire amount to artists who were in need of support. Under the Aikyam establishment, she provides scholarship to 15 impoverished school children for their academics and also trains them in dance. She has been honoured with 'women empowerment award' for the upliftment of girl children.

Ten years through her career as a performer, she has rendered performances in several prestigious festivals in India and abroad and part of several renowned productions. She also conducts workshops. She is a district player in badminton sport. A district topper in academics and acquainted in Rangoli making. She is also a homemaker and happily married with a child who keeps her busy.

9 798889 322715